50 p

Crochet by Design

Crochet by Design

Wynne Broughton

Pitman Publishing

First published 1976
PITMAN PUBLISHING
Pitman House, 39 Parker Street, London WC2B 5PB

SIR ISAAC PITMAN AND SONS LTD
PO Box 46038, Banda Street, Nairobi, Kenya

PITMAN PUBISHING PTY LTD
Pitman House, 158 Bouverie Street, Carlton, Victoria 3053,
Australia

PITMAN PUBLISHING CORPORATION
6 East 43 Street, New York, NY 10017, USA

PITMAN PUBLISHING
COPP CLARK PUBLISHING
517 Wellington Street West, Toronto M5V 1GL

ISBN 0 273 00477 8

Text set in 11/12 pt Photon Baskerville, printed by photolithography,
and bound in Great Britain at The Pitman Press, Bath
G6015:16

This book is dedicated to Jean Morton, producer of Associated Television's *Women Today* programmes, with sincere thanks for her natural charm and relaxed presence which made all my appearances in *Crochet Party* so 'butterfly-free' and easy.

WYNNE BROUGHTON

Preface

Crochet by Design aims to give scope to the creative urge and artistic inclinations of the individualist. By following the few simple rules, clearly and concisely described and illustrated here, the phrase 'all my own work' may be applied truthfully, from the initial inspiration to the completed article.

Crochet today has reached a peak of fashion never before enjoyed by this ancient, fascinating and versatile handicraft. It is the one leisure occupation which requires only a single tool, the hook, to produce anything from a small table mat to a glamorous gown; and it can be done in a cosy sitting room, when travelling, or during a few spare minutes available in the day. Another of its great attributes is that, unlike knitting, there is no clickety-click to offend the ears of other company present!

Throughout the world, designers who appreciate the endless potential variations on the few basic stitches of crochet are continually producing instructions for simple or elaborate fashionwear and distinctive articles for the home.

In these push-button days, the tendency to copy rather than originate is all too apparent; but it can be devastating to spend hours in working a widely distributed pattern and then see someone else wearing, or using, an identical article. A little extra time spent in personalizing by design not only eliminates this possibility but cannot fail to fill the do-it-yourself designer with tremendous pride.

Before attempting to design, it is essential for the worker to be thoroughly conversant with the basic stitches and rules of crochet, and to understand correct tension and pattern reading. For the enthusiastic beginner, or the person who wishes to know more about the handicraft, everything necessary is included later in this book. General information about equipment, choice of yarns, making up and after care is also provided.

The middle section of the book caters for those who have no time, or inclination, to design. Included here is a wide selection of patterns for working fashion garments, children's wear, toys, and lovely things for the home.

Contents

Acknowledgements

Lister & Co, (Knitting Wools) Ltd, Wakefield
Abel Morrall Ltd, Redditch—Hooks and hairpins
Pauline Howard, Bramcote, Nottingham—Line drawings
J. & P. Coats Ltd, Glasgow
Woman's Realm magazine—Jacket designed by Elizabeth Collins
Hayfield Wools: Susan Shanks & Partners—Bikini
Woman & Home magazine—Tunisian Tunic
Woman's Weekly magazine—Floppity clown

Part 1
Design

General procedure

As the revival of crochet in the mid-60s has been attributed mainly to its elegant application to the fashion scene, it seems appropriate to begin with this important facet of the handicraft. It must not be forgotten, however, that it has also made a great impact on the domestic front. More about this will follow later.

All the designs cover a wide field, from which other ideas will soon develop. Do not be afraid to draw. It is not necessary to be an artist but drawings are a great help, and ability comes easily with practice.

Estimation of yarn requirements is, perhaps, a more tricky stage in crochet design. Unless access to unlimited supplies of yarn is available, or a kindly shopkeeper will put aside approximate needs for a reasonable time, thus allowing the designer to circumvent the actual working out, then a certain amount of drawing and arithmetical calculation is unavoidable. It is an encouraging fact that as more variations on the basic themes are designed, the easier and more fascinating the whole exercise becomes.

Before tackling any design, it is essential to have at the finger-tips a good knowledge of the basic stitches, rules and tools of crochet. For those who have yet to acquire this, a study of pages 127 to 144, coupled with a little serious practical work, will provide all the necessary information.

EQUIPMENT
Sketch pad.
Graph paper, marked in tenths.
Plain drawing paper.
Notebook.
Pencils—1 medium hard, 1 soft, lead.
Ball-point pen, fine.
Tape-measure (fibreglass or similar non-stretch) marked in centimetres and inches.
Two rulers, preferably transparent, marked 30 cm (12 in.) and 15 cm (6 in.).

Set of crochet hooks, ideally similar to those pictured on page 130.

Oddments of yarn in various thicknesses for experiments.

A metric conversion table translating centimetres to inches.

Scissors—keep a really sharp pair always at hand.

Needles—blunt-ended tapestry needles are best for making up. A selection of these, together with a variety of ordinary sewing needles and several bodkins, should be available.

Pins—good-quality steel pins with small, possibly coloured knobs should be kept in a separate container to needles.

Small safety pins are useful for marking work.

Thimble—the much-despised thimble saves many an injured finger during sewing up.

A steam iron or good plain iron should be available.

Ironing board—a well-padded, clean and reasonably wide board will accommodate any crochet work.

Cloth for pressing—a clean piece of fine cotton material measuring about a yard or a metre square should be kept specially for this purpose.

Sleeve board—useful, but not essential.

YARN

The word yarn covers the whole range of threads, from the finest cottons to the thickest of wools and synthetics.

Today, more than ever before, there is a yarn to suit everything and everybody in reliably fast colours: fine cottons and all other types of yarn have reached a degree of near-perfection such as our forbears never dreamed of.

Yarns are classified into two main groups—the natural fibres such as cottons and pure wool, and the man-made varieties such as nylon, Courtelle, metallics and others. A third group consists of mixtures of any natural and synthetic fibres.

Some people are misled by the term 'ply', which does not necessarily refer to the thickness of the yarn. In fact, one 2-ply can be thicker than another 3-ply of different manufacture or processing. It is therefore imperative to give careful consideration to the type of yarn to be used in any design, and, when following a printed pattern, to use the recommended material. Substitution can sometimes lead to disaster, or at least to disappointment in the finished article.

The crêpe wools and synthetics lend themselves very well to crochet work, being well twisted and therefore not so prone to splitting by hook action. Yarns of a more loosely twisted type, however, usually produce garments of a softer texture, and are therefore more suitable for garments which will be in close contact with sensitive skins. Garments worked in pure wool are recommended by most people for sportswear, but for really hard wear the synthetics and mixtures are difficult to beat. It is often impossible to break the threads by hand.

The importance of buying sufficient yarn of the same dye lot

4

to complete the work in hand cannot be over emphasized. Even in these days of technological skills, dyes do inevitably vary from lot to lot; a fact which will show all too clearly if a later purchase has to be made, when the heartbreaking tide-mark appears, usually in the most obvious position!

METRICATION

Until metrication is well established, there is bound to be some confusion as to amounts of yarn required, particularly when working from older patterns.

Most shop assistants will translate ounces into grammes, but the calculation is not very difficult. The following is a quick method which is satisfactory for most needs, unless strict accuracy is essential:

$$1 \ \text{oz} = 28 \cdot 347 \ \text{gm exactly}$$
$$1 \ \text{oz} = 28 \ \text{gm (approx)}$$
$$1\tfrac{1}{2} \ \text{oz} = 40 \ \text{gm (approx)}$$
$$1\tfrac{3}{4} \ \text{oz} = 50 \ \text{gm (approx)}$$
$$3\tfrac{1}{2} \ \text{oz} = 100 \ \text{gm (approx)}$$

The following quick-conversion table will save any arithmetic:

IMPERIAL (1-oz balls)	METRIC (50-gm balls)
1	1
1 or 2	no change
3 or 4	1 less
5 or 6	2 less
7 to 9	3 less
10 or 11	4 less
12 or 13	5 less
14 to 16	6 less
17 or 18	7 less
19 or 20	8 less
21 to 23	9 less
24 or 25	10 less
26 or 27	11 less
28 or 29	12 less
30 to 32	13 less

Since not all yarns are made up into 50-gm balls the following table gives alternative requirements in the case of 20- and 25-gm balls for 1-oz balls:

Ounces	20-gm balls	25-gm balls
1	2	2
2	3	3
5	8	6
10	15	12

ESTIMATING YARN REQUIREMENT FOR A NEW DESIGN

Several methods of calculating yarn requirements have been evolved by the author, as follows:

1. The 1-ball stitch or pattern count comparison

This is suitable when working plain pieces of fabric (that is, without much shaping) in one stitch, say double crochet or trebles.

One whole ball is worked according to the stitch, or pattern, designed. From this the number of stitches or patterns in each row is counted and multiplied by the number of rows worked. This gives the total number of stitches or patterns in the complete test piece.

The number of rows required to make the whole piece in the design is then worked out. This is multiplied by the number of stitches in each row. The resultant figure is then divided by the number of stitches in the test piece, which gives the number of balls required for that piece of work.

Note: This method is used for the back of the square-motif jacket (page 17).

2. The 1-ball length test

This is used when working in several colours, as for the Old American squares for the jacket (page 14).

The length of one whole ball is measured in centimetres or inches. This is divided by the length used in a test piece, or pieces, thus giving the number of pieces that can be worked with one ball.

The total number of pieces required is then worked out, and this figure is divided by the number produced by one ball. The result is the total estimated consumption.

3. The 1-ball comparison by graph test

The complete article is drawn to scale on graph paper. Adjacent to this the complete 1-ball test piece is drawn to scale, as shown for the mother's and daughter's dresses in Fig. 11.

The total number of squares and part-squares on the full drawing is divided by the total number of squares on the test piece. The result is the amount of yarn required to complete the work.

Note: A certain amount of eye-straining counting of squares can be avoided by cutting out the whole-graph test piece, placing it over the complete diagram, where it fits in its entirety, and marking its boundaries with broken or coloured lines. The odd squares and part squares outside these lines are then counted up and divided by the number of test-piece squares. This figure is then added to the number of complete-ball sections, giving the total requirement.

When counting squares on actual graph paper, it will be noticed that the complete 100-square blocks are marked by a dark line, and the 25-square blocks also appear in a slightly heavier line than the tiny squares.

4. The sectional 1-ball weight test

A convenient number of sections or motifs is worked. These are weighed and worked out to individual weight. This figure is divided into the weight of one whole ball, the result giving the number of pieces that can be made from this ball.

The total number of similar pieces or motifs is then calculated and divided by the number each ball will make; the result being the number of balls required. (See motif dress, page 23).

5. The 1-piece calculated-guess test

This calculation eliminates most of the arithmetic involved in methods 1 to 4, and with a little experience reasonable accuracy can be achieved quickly. It is most appropriate where straight edges or very little shaping are required.

One whole piece or a section of a piece of the design is worked, and the amount of yarn consumed is recorded. This piece is then taken in comparison with the other pieces, and the total requirement is assessed. (See the 6-hour waistcoat, page 32.)

6. The 1-ball full-size pattern test

This method also saves some of the arithmetical calculations.

A full-size pattern of the article to be made is drawn on paper (old newspapers or wallpaper are useful for this purpose). The test piece with one ball is worked, and drawn twice on paper, adjacent to the whole drawing.

The test drawings are cut out; one is left whole, the other is divided into one half, one quarter and one eighth of the whole. The whole cut-out test is then fitted wherever possible over the full-size pattern, and its boundaries are marked by coloured or broken lines. The other smaller test sections are placed jig-saw fashion over the remaining uncovered sections, and their boundaries are similarly marked. All the sections are added together, giving the total requirement.

Note: All quantities given in the ensuing patterns are based on average requirements, and are therefore approximate.

SELECTING THE STITCHES

With endless possibilities of stitch combinations, the enthusiastic designer should have no difficulty in choosing from established patterns and adapting them, or in working out others.

When designing, care should be taken to centre the pattern where possible, so that it falls symmetrically on each side. This can be done either by placing the exact middle of the pattern at dead centre, or by placing one pattern on each side of centre.

When a garment is designed in a pattern which covers several stitches, each row should begin and end with either a complete pattern or half a pattern. Thus, when the pieces are seamed together, complete patterns are formed. Where increases for shapings are made at the beginning and end of rows, extra stitches are often more conveniently made in double crochet, treble, or other basic stitches to suit the pattern, until sufficient stitches have been added to form an extra pattern.

Test pieces should be lightly pressed, where yarn instructions advise this.

Crocheted garments should never be hung in a wardrobe; it is better to keep them in an uncluttered drawer where it is unlikely that they will suffer creasing. Nevertheless, allowance for 'drop' should be made when designing, particularly in the case of dresses and jackets made in heavier yarns. When a garment drops too far, the instructions for shortening, on page 142 will provide the answer to the problem.

STAGES IN DESIGNING

The following is a guide to each stage in design. It will vary sometimes according to the article to be made and the method of yarn estimation adopted.

1. Take and record correct measurements. In the case of garments, add movement allowances as necessary.

2. Select yarn to be used. Note the weight or length of each ball.

3. Devise or select the stitch or stitch combination to be worked.

4. Plan the design, drawing a rough sketch if it is felt this will be helpful. See suit, page 42.

5. Work a small test piece, or pieces, to determine size of hook, or hooks, to be used. Measure this for tension and record result.

6. Work out from the test piece the number of stitches required to begin each section of the work, the position of the shapings and any other relevant details.

7. Make another test piece, this time using one whole ball from beginning to end, working over the number of stitches calculated in stage 6 for one piece of the work.

8. Draw the design to scale or full size on graph paper or plain paper as desired.

9. Measure test piece prepared in stage 7 (after light pressing if necessary) and, if appropriate to the method being used, draw this to scale alongside a drawing of the whole article.

10. Work out total yarn requirement.

11. Write out instructions in detail.

12. Work out and make up the design.

13. Photograph the finished product, if desired.
14. File all details carefully for future reference.

Note: At first glance the above methods may seem rather complicated, but in practice they are all very simple, and come easily after the first design has been accomplished.

In all the final yarn-requirement calculations, parts of a ball must be taken to the next nearest ball.

SIZES

There is only one way to ensure exact sizing of any crocheted article, and that is to work throughout to correct measurements and perfect tension. See notes on tension, page 129.

To cover the transition period between the departure from the British scene of inches and the arrival of centimetres, both units are used in this book.

It is essential to know the correct method of taking personal measurements before beginning to design a garment, whether it is to be for a baby, an older child, or a person of average, small, medium, or larger than usual dimensions. The human frame, from tiny baby to adult, does not always conform to the average sizes adopted of necessity by our fashion houses. For the purpose of self-comparison, it may perhaps be useful to know the standard measurements, some of which are listed here.
Extract from the Measurement Chart approved by the Measurement Standard Committee of the Pattern Fashion Industry, giving approximate equivalent measurements in centimetres and inches.

Girls (for the girl who has not yet begun to mature)

Size	10		12		14	
	cm	in.	cm	in.	cm	in.
Breast	72·5	28·5	76·0	30·0	81·0	32·0
Waist	62·0	24·5	64·5	25·5	67·0	26·5
Hip	76·0	30·0	81·0	32·0	86·5	34·0
Back waist length	32·0	12·75	34·0	13·5	36·0	14·25
Height (approx)	142·0	56·0	148·5	58·5	155·0	61·0

Misses (for a well-proportioned and developed figure)

Size	8		10		12	
	cm	in.	cm	in.	cm	in.
Bust	80·0	31·5	82·5	32·5	86·0	34·0
Waist	58·5	23·0	61·0	24·0	64·0	25·5
Hip	85·0	33·5	87·5	34·5	91·5	36·0
Back waist length	40·0	15·75	40·5	16·0	41·0	16·25

Size	14		16		18	
	cm	in.	cm	in.	cm	in.
Bust	91·5	36·0	96·5	38·0	101·5	40·0
Waist	68·5	27·0	73·75	29·0	78·75	31·0
Hip	96·5	38·0	101·5	40·0	106·5	42·0
Back waist length	42·0	16·5	42·5	16·75	43·0	17·0

Size	20	
	cm	in.
Bust	106·5	42·0
Waist	83·5	33·0
Hip	111·5	44·0
Back waist length	43·75	17·25

Women (for the larger, more fully matured figure)

Size	38		40		42	
	cm	in.	cm	in.	cm	in.
Bust	106·5	42·0	111·5	44·0	117·0	46·0
Waist	86·5	34·0	91·5	36·0	96·5	38·0
Hip	111·5	44·0	117·0	46·0	122·0	48·0
Back waist length	43·5	17·25	44·0	17·38	44·25	17·5

Men

Size	38		40		42	
	cm	in.	cm	in.	cm	in.
Chest	96·5	38·0	102·5	40·0	107·0	42·0
Waist	81·0	32·0	86·5	34·0	91·5	36·0
Hip (seat)	99·0	39·0	104·0	41·0	109·0	43·0
Neck	38·0	15·0	39·5	15·5	40·5	16·0

Measuring children

Measure around the breast, not too snugly. Toddler sizes are designed for a figure between that of a baby and a child.

Toddlers

Size	0·5		1		2	
	cm	in.	cm	in.	cm	in.
Breast	48·0	19·0	50·5	20·0	53·0	21·0
Waist	48·0	19·0	49·5	19·5	50·5	20·0
Length	43·0	17·0	45·5	18·0	48·0	19·0

Children

Size	3		4		5	
	cm	in.	cm	in.	cm	in.
Breast	56·0	22·0	58·5	23·0	61·0	24·0
Waist	52·0	20·5	53·5	21·0	54·5	21·5
Hip	58·5	23·0	61·0	24·0	63·5	25·0
Back waist length	23·0	9·0	24·0	9·5	25·5	10·0
Height (approx)	94·0	37·0	101·5	40·0	109·0	43·0

Personal measurement chart

The chart for recording measurements, taken in conjunction with the two figure drawings (Fig. 1), provides a clear and simple method of taking measurements. If details are written in pencil, they may be easily erased in favour of other figures. It is advisable to remeasure at least once a year. When taking the more awkward measurements, the assistance of a friend can be very useful.

Movement allowance, where necessary, should be added to the actual figures when taking masurements. Slacken the tape slightly, at least 2·5–5·0 cm (1–2 in.), over bust and hips for the average adult figure. For the fuller figure a little more should be allowed, as skimpy garments tend to give the illusion of even greater proportions.

Some crocheted garments, particularly dresses made in the heavier yarns, do tend to drop a little. Allowance of 2·5–5·0 cm (1–2 in.) should be made in length.

Always check the measurements given by friends for their own garments. The once proud possessor of a 90–62–95 cm (36–24–38 in.) figure is sometimes found guilty of revelling in the nostalgic illusion of former days; the actual reading may be 100–77–106 cm (40–31–42 in.)!

Good foundation garments and a plain well-fitting underslip should be worn when measurements are being taken, and unless the dress is of very fine texture, this should be removed.

Measurement chart

Date . . . .

		cm	*in.*

A–B Bust.
C–D Waist.
E–F Hips (22 cm or 9 in. below natural waist).
G–H Across back (below shoulders and 10 cm or 4 in. below base of neck).

J–K Shoulder length; neck base to top of arm.

K–L Front length from neck base over bust to waist.

M–N Back neck to waist.

P–Q–R–S Front; natural waist to hem.

W–X–Y–Z Back; natural waist to hem.

1–2 Sleeve; shoulder to elbow crook.

2–3 Sleeve; elbow to wrist.

4–5 Sleeve; underarm to wrist.

6–7 Neck; all round.

8–9 Arm; all round (2·5 cm or 1 in. below armpit).

10–11 Arm; all round above elbow for short sleeves.

12 Wrist; all round.

Fig. 1. How to take measurements.

ABBREVIATIONS

The following list gives the more usual terms used in crochet, with their relevant abbreviations in the second column. The American terms and abbreviations, where they differ from the English, appear immediately below the English, in italics.

Term	Abbreviation
alternate	alt
approximate(ly)	approx
begin(ning)	beg
block(s)	blk(s)
Bobble(s)	B(s)
centimetre(s)	cm
chain	ch
cluster(s)	cl(s)
colour	col
continue	cont
contrast 1, 2, etc.	C1, C2, etc.
decrease(ing)	dec
double crochet	dc
single crochet	*sc*
double treble	dbl tr
treble crochet	*tr*
follow(ing)	foll
foundation chain	f ch
gramme(s)	gm
group	gp
half treble	hlf tr
half double crochet	*half dc*
inch(es)	in.
increase(ing)	inc
loop(s)	lp(s)
main colour	M
metre(s)	m
number(s)	no(s)
ounce(s)	oz
pattern(s)	patt(s)
picot(s)	pct(s)
quadruple treble	quad tr
quintuple treble	quin tr
remain(ing)	rem
repeat	rep
shell	sh
slip stitch	ss
space(s)	sp(s)
starting chain	st ch
stitch(es)	st(s)
together	tog
treble	tr
double crochet	*dc*
triple treble	trip tr
double treble	*dbl tr*
turning chain(s)	t ch(s)

wool round hook	wrh
yarn over	*yo*
yarn over hook	yoh

* means repeat the instructions following the number of times stated, i.e. in addition to carrying out the instruction in the first place.

( ) means repeat contents of brackets the number of times stated.

When various sizes are given in a pattern, those in brackets refer to the larger sizes.

The first design: a jacket

Now that the bread-and-butter course is thoroughly digested, we can prepare for the cake. Do not be too ambitious at first. A simple article, well made to correct dimensions, will give confidence for more elaborate work later.

What shall I make? This decision is a very personal one, which may include anything from a baby's dress to a set of chairbacks. As a 'starter' in this book, the popular any-length jacket has been chosen. If this idea does not have universal appeal, the designs appearing later will, it is hoped, attract potential designers and lead to many lovely personalized creations.

The jacket (see plate 1) uses the Old American or 'Grannie' square motif. A loosely fitting jacket of this type, with treble-stitch back and motif fronts, is always useful and easy to pop on and off according to changes in temperature. It gives the designer practice in working out both motif and one-row pattern formation, and in estimating yarn requirements, in preparation for more intricate work later.

If desired, the whole jacket may be designed in motifs. Also, by the addition or subtraction of rows of motifs and the corresponding treatment of the back, the jacket may be lengthened or shortened as required. Designed with no fastenings, the jacket will fit a range of sizes from bust 86·0 cm (34 in.) to 97·0 cm (38 in.).

Note: In all crochet design, a certain number of calculations are inevitable. Do not be put off by the arithmetic involved; it is all really very elementary.

MEASUREMENTS
Bust 96·0 cm (38 in.)
Hips 102·0 cm (40 in.)
Width across back 45·0 cm (17·75 in.)
Length 64·0 cm (25 in.)

YARN

The motif is usually worked in two or more colours. Each square can be made in the same colour combination, or every one can be different, according to the artistic inclination of the worker and the availability of yarn. When the jacket illustrated was made, there were so many oddments of double-crêpe wool in the workbox that it seemed opportune to apply at least some of them to good use. When working with oddments of yarn, however, it is very important to ensure that the same quality of material is used throughout, otherwise perfect symmetry, so essential to a professional finish, will not be achieved.

It is quite satisfactory to make the two jacket fronts entirely of square motifs, but in order to add a little shaping to the neckline one triangular matching motif can be inserted at each side, giving a much better fit.

When changing colour at the beginning of a round, break off the yarn at the end of the last round, then join in the new colour to the next corner space. If using the same colour for more than one round, work slip-stitches into each treble, one slip-stitch into the next space, then follow instructions.

THE MOTIF FOR THE FRONT

Motifs can be made in many shapes and sizes; the Old American (Grannie) square (see plate 2) is probably the oldest, yet it is still among the most popular today. Instructions for making it may vary slightly, but those given below are very satisfactory, the resulting squares being evenly formed and lying perfectly flat.

Note: Each of the first four rounds begins with 3 chain, representing the first treble stitch of the group. In the following instructions this is referred to as a treble in the first group.

To make the motif
Begin with 6ch, join to first ch with 1ss.
1st round 3ch (for first tr), 2tr into ring, 3ch, (3tr 3ch into ring) 3 times, join to 3rd of 3ch with 1ss.
2nd round * (3tr 3ch 3tr) into 3 ch sp, 1ch, rep from * 3 times; join to top of first st with 1ss.
3rd round * (3tr 3ch 3tr) in 3ch sp, 1ch, 3tr in 1ch sp, 1ch, rep from * 3 times; join to first st with 1ss.
4th round * (3tr 3ch 3tr) in to 3ch sp (for corner), 1ch, 3tr in next sp, 1ch, 3tr in next sp, 1ch, rep from * 3 times; join to first st with 1ss.
For further rounds of 3tr groups following 4th round, work an extra 3tr group along each side.
5th round 1dc into each st, 3dc into each corner. Fasten off.

To make the triangle or half-square
Using colours to match the sequence of the square, begin with 6ch, join into a ring with 1ss.

Now continue working in *rows* not rounds until the 5th round.

1st row 4ch, then into ring work 3tr, 3ch, 3tr, 1ch, 1tr, 4ch, turn.

2nd row 3tr into 1ch sp, 1ch, (3tr 3ch 3tr) into 3ch sp for corner, 1ch, 3tr in 4ch sp at beginning of previous row, 1ch, 1tr, 4ch, turn.

3rd row (3tr 1ch) twice, (3tr 3ch 3tr) into 3ch sp for corner, (1ch 3tr) twice, 1ch, 1tr, 4ch, turn.

4th row As 2nd row, but working an extra 3tr group into each 1ch sp between groups of previous row.

For further rows following 4th row, work an extra 3tr group along the sides, as required to match the square.

5th round Work 1dc into each st, 3dc at each corner. Fasten off.

The motif test

Scraps of wool are used for rounds 1 and 2 in the same colour, and for rounds 3 and 4 in the same colour, giving a floral effect. As will be seen in plate 1, every motif is of a different colour combination. Round 5 is worked in the main colour, i.e. the one planned for the entire back of the jacket.

If every motif is to be worked in exactly the same colours, the amounts required must be calculated accordingly.

Three motif tests must now be made to decide which produces the correct size and tension.

Using first a No. 4·50 hook, then a 4·00, and lastly a 3·50, make one motif of each size. The one which appeared most satisfactory as to texture and size to combine with the plain back of the jacket illustrated was that worked on the 4·00 hook, as follows:

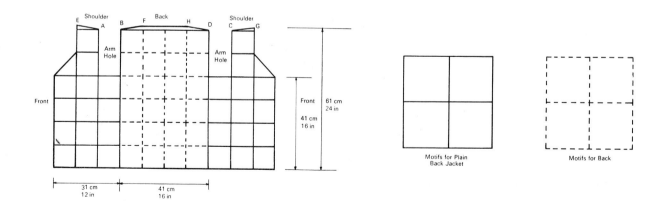

Fig. 2. Positioning the motifs for the jacket.

16

Measurement	10·0 cm (4 in.) square
Length of yarn used for rounds 1 and 2	4·5 m (5 yd approx)
Length of yarn used for rounds 3 and 4	9·0 m (10 yd approx) i.e. exactly double rounds 1 and 2
Length of yarn used for round 5	4·0 m (4·33 yd) i.e. 1 m for every 10 cm dc worked

Figure 2 shows the jacket lying flat before the shoulder seams are joined, giving the exact position of the motifs and plain back. Twenty-eight motifs and two triangles comprise the fronts, and for the purposes of yarn estimation, the triangles are treated as one motif.

Assuming that one whole new ball of the main-colour wool measures 70·0 m (76 yd approx), yarn requirement for the motifs will be as follows if all the motifs are the same:

1st contrast, rounds 1 and 2: 4·5 × 29 m = 130·5 m or 2 balls (approx).

2nd contrast rounds 3 and 4: 9·0 × 29 m = 261·0 m or 4 balls (approx).

Main colour, round 5: 4·0 × 29 m = 116·0 m (to be added to the main colour for back and edgings).

THE PLAIN BACK

Choice of stitch
For the plain back, continuous rows of treble stitches are appropriate, to correspond with those of the motifs.

Yarn
Double-crêpe wool in 25-gm balls was chosen for the main colour of the jacket illustrated, and the same yarn was used for the 5th round of all squares and triangles, and for the all-round double-crochet edging of jacket and armholes.

The No. 4·00 hook chosen for the motifs was also used for the back.

First test for tension of back
With a No 4·00 hook a sample was worked over 24 treble stitches for 12 rows. After light pressing, on careful measurement the tension was:

4tr = 2·5 cm (1 in.)
2 rows = 2·5 cm (1 in.)
Number of stitches required for back measurement of 41 cm (16 in.) = 64.
Number of rows for length of 61 cm (24 in.), excluding edgings = 48.

Second test for yarn requirement of main colour
Using a whole ball of main colour and the No 4·00 hook,

another test piece was worked, this time over 64 treble stitches, which constitutes the whole back width. The ball ran out at the end of the twelfth row. Result:

Number of tr sts worked from ball was $64 \times 12 = 768$.
Number of tr sts to be worked on whole back, i.e. 48 rows plus 1 row neck shaping (49 rows) is therefore $64 \times 49 = 3136$.
Yarn required for back (70 m per ball) is therefore 3136 divided by $768 = 4.08$ balls.

SUMMARY OF YARN REQUIRED
Main colour:

Back		4·08 balls
Yarn for 29 5th-round motifs	116·0 m	
2 rounds dc each armhole	20·4 m	
2 rounds dc jacket edging	50·0 m	
	186·4 m	= 2·60 balls
		6·68 balls (say 7 balls)

Therefore total amount of main colour	= 7 balls
Contrasts:	
Total amount required of first contrast	= 2 balls
Total amount required of second contrast	= 4 balls
Total yarn requirement	13 balls

Note: If the back is worked entirely in motifs, as indicated by the broken lines in Fig. 2, the main colour yarn requirement will be reduced by 4·08 balls and the amounts required for the motifs will be increased proportionately.

Similarly, if the jacket is to be made shorter or longer, adjustments in quantities must be calculated.

Now, at last, after the sums, practical work can begin. Write or type the full instructions as follows.

TO MAKE THE JACKET
Measurements: as on page 14
Materials: main colour—Lister Lavenda double-crêpe wool

25-gm balls	7 balls
1st contrast	2 balls
2nd contrast	4 balls

Tension: each motif measures 10·0 cm (4 in.) square
for the back $4\text{tr} = 2.5$ cm (1 in.)
$2\text{ rows} = 2.5$ cm (1 in.)
Abbreviations: see full list, page 13.

The front
Work 28 motifs and two triangles as instructed on pages 15 to 16; rounds 1 and 2 in first contrast yarn, rounds 3 and 4 in second contrast, and round 5 in main colour. Work 3dc into each corner of the 5th round; fasten off all ends neatly. Press lightly

Measurement	10·0 cm (4 in.) square
Length of yarn used for rounds 1 and 2	4·5 m (5 yd approx)
Length of yarn used for rounds 3 and 4	9·0 m (10 yd approx) i.e. exactly double rounds 1 and 2
Length of yarn used for round 5	4·0 m (4·33 yd) i.e. 1 m for every 10 cm dc worked

Figure 2 shows the jacket lying flat before the shoulder seams are joined, giving the exact position of the motifs and plain back. Twenty-eight motifs and two triangles comprise the fronts, and for the purposes of yarn estimation, the triangles are treated as one motif.

Assuming that one whole new ball of the main-colour wool measures 70·0 m (76 yd approx), yarn requirement for the motifs will be as follows if all the motifs are the same:

1st contrast, rounds 1 and 2: 4·5 × 29 m = 130·5 m or 2 balls (approx).

2nd contrast rounds 3 and 4: 9·0 × 29 m = 261·0 m or 4 balls (approx).

Main colour, round 5: 4·0 × 29 m = 116·0 m (to be added to the main colour for back and edgings).

THE PLAIN BACK

Choice of stitch
For the plain back, continuous rows of treble stitches are appropriate, to correspond with those of the motifs.

Yarn
Double-crêpe wool in 25-gm balls was chosen for the main colour of the jacket illustrated, and the same yarn was used for the 5th round of all squares and triangles, and for the all-round double-crochet edging of jacket and armholes.

The No. 4·00 hook chosen for the motifs was also used for the back.

First test for tension of back
With a No 4·00 hook a sample was worked over 24 treble stitches for 12 rows. After light pressing, on careful measurement the tension was:

4 tr = 2·5 cm (1 in.)

2 rows = 2·5 cm (1 in.)

Number of stitches required for back measurement of 41 cm (16 in.) = 64.

Number of rows for length of 61 cm (24 in.), excluding edgings = 48.

Second test for yarn requirement of main colour
Using a whole ball of main colour and the No 4·00 hook,

another test piece was worked, this time over 64 treble stitches, which constitutes the whole back width. The ball ran out at the end of the twelfth row. Result:

Number of tr sts worked from ball was $64 \times 12 = 768$.

Number of tr sts to be worked on whole back, i.e. 48 rows plus 1 row neck shaping (49 rows) is therefore $64 \times 49 = 3136$.

Yarn required for back (70 m per ball) is therefore 3136 divided by $768 = 4.08$ balls.

SUMMARY OF YARN REQUIRED
Main colour:

Back		4.08 balls
Yarn for 29 5th-round motifs	116.0 m	
2 rounds dc each armhole	20.4 m	
2 rounds dc jacket edging	50.0 m	
	186.4 m	= 2.60 balls
		6.68 balls (say 7 balls)

Therefore total amount of main colour	= 7 balls
Contrasts:	
Total amount required of first contrast	= 2 balls
Total amount required of second contrast	= 4 balls
Total yarn requirement	13 balls

Note: If the back is worked entirely in motifs, as indicated by the broken lines in Fig. 2, the main colour yarn requirement will be reduced by 4.08 balls and the amounts required for the motifs will be increased proportionately.

Similarly, if the jacket is to be made shorter or longer, adjustments in quantities must be calculated.

Now, at last, after the sums, practical work can begin. Write or type the full instructions as follows.

TO MAKE THE JACKET
Measurements: as on page 14
Materials: main colour—Lister Lavenda double-crêpe wool

25-gm balls	7 balls
1st contrast	2 balls
2nd contrast	4 balls

Tension: each motif measures 10.0 cm (4 in.) square
for the back 4tr = 2.5 cm (1 in.)
2 rows = 2.5 cm (1 in.)
Abbreviations: see full list, page 13.

The front
Work 28 motifs and two triangles as instructed on pages 15 to 16; rounds 1 and 2 in first contrast yarn, rounds 3 and 4 in second contrast, and round 5 in main colour. Work 3dc into each corner of the 5th round; fasten off all ends neatly. Press lightly

on wrong side following the instructions on the ball band. Sew or crochet the motifs together as in Fig. 2.

Shoulder shaping. Join main colour to top of shoulder motif at point A in Fig. 2. Work 1dc into each of next 10 sts, 1tr into every st to point E. Break off yarn.

For the second shoulder shaping, join main colour to top of shoulder at C, work 1dc into each of next 10sts, 1tr into each st to G. Break off yarn.

The back
This is worked in one straight piece, the armhole being formed by motifs.

Begin with 65ch.

1st row 1tr into 3rd ch from hook, 1tr into every ch to end, 3ch, turn (64sts).

2nd row 1tr into next st, 1tr into every st to end, 3ch, turn.

3rd to 48th rows inclusive Rep 2nd row, omitting 3ch at the turn on 48th row, turn.

49th row 1dc into each of next 10sts, 1tr into each of next 44sts, 1dc into each of next 10sts. Fasten off.

Press lightly on wrong side.

TO MAKE UP
Join shoulder seams, placing A to B and E to F for one side, and C to D and G to H on the other.

Work 2 rounds dc evenly round each armhole. Work 2 rounds dc evenly all round jacket, making 3dc into each corner. Fasten off.

Press shoulder seams and edgings very lightly on wrong side.

Square motifs

Gay and versatile as it is, the Old American square will not appeal to all designers, and experimenting with motifs can be great fun.

Several alternative squares appear on pages 19 to 21. These can be adapted for use in the jacket, or made into an endless variety of things, some suggestions for which are given in Figs. 3 and 4. No doubt the enthusiastic designer will quickly be able to invent others of equal or greater attraction.

Remember, the size of any motif can be increased or decreased by the use of different types of yarn, different sized hooks, or the addition or subtraction of rounds to produce the required size. Pretty variations can be achieved by replacing some treble groups with clusters or bobbles, or other stitch combinations.

THE POSY SQUARE
This motif looks attractive worked in two colours, or the

shade of the flower can be alternated with others. (See plate 3.)
Using the first colour, begin with 5ch, join into a ring with 1ss.

1st round   5ch, (1tr into circle, 2ch) 7 times, join into 3rd of 5ch with 1ss (8 sps).

2nd round   For petals, (1dc, 1hlf tr, 3tr, 1hlf tr, 1dc) into next sp, 8 times, break off yarn.

3rd round   Join in second colour, (1ss into back of first dc of next petal, 5ch) 8 times, join into first ss of round with 1ss.

4th round   1ss into next sp, into same sp for first corner work (4ch, 1–2dtr cl, 4ch, 1–3dtr cl, 3ch), into next sp work * 4dbl tr, 3ch, into next sp for next corner, work (1–3dbl tr cl, 4ch, 1–3dbl tr cl, 3ch), rep from *twice, 4dbl tr into next sp, 3ch, join to top of first cl with 1ss.

5th round   1ss into next (corner) sp, 4ch, 1–2dbl tr cl into same sp, 4ch, 1–3dbl tr cl into same sp, 2ch, * 3 dbl tr into next sp, 1dbl tr into each of next 4dbl tr, 3dbl tr into next sp, 2ch, 1–3dbl tr cl into next corner sp, 4ch, 1–3dbl tr cl into same sp, 2ch, rep from * twice, 3dbl tr in next sp, 1dbl tr into each of next 4dbl tr, 3dbl tr into next sp, 2ch, join to top of first cl with 1ss. Fasten off.

THE ROUNDABOUT SQUARE

For an illustration of this motif, see plate 4. Begin with 6ch, join into a ring with 1ss.

1st round   7ch, (1 dbl tr into ring, 3ch) 7 times (8 spokes), join to 4th of 7ch with 1ss.

2nd round   Ss into next sp, 3ch, 3tr into same sp, 3ch, (4tr into next sp, 3ch) 7 times, join to top of 3ch with 1ss.

3rd round   Ss into next sp, into same sp work (3ch, 2tr, 1ch, 3tr), 1ch, (3tr, 1ch, 3tr) into next sp, 3ch, (3tr, 1ch, 3tr) into next sp, 1ch, * (3tr, 1ch, 3tr) into next sp, 3ch (3tr, 1ch, 3tr) into next sp, 1ch, rep from * once, (3tr, 1ch, 3tr) into next sp, 3ch, join to top of 3ch with 1ss.

4th round   Ss to next 1ch sp, * 1dc into same sp, 3ch, 1dc into next sp, 3ch, 1dc into next sp, 3ch, (2tr, 3ch, 2tr) into next (corner) sp, 3ch, rep from * 3 times, join to first dc with 1ss. Fasten off.

CROSSROADS MOTIF

For an illustration of this motif, see plate 5.
Begin with 6ch, join into ring with 1ss.

1st round   Into ring work (3ch, 1tr, 2ch, 1–2tr cl, 4ch), (1–2tr cl, 2ch, 1–2tr cl, 4ch) into ring 3 times, join to top of 3ch with 1ss.

2nd round   1ss to next 2ch sp, 3ch, 2tr in same sp, 2ch, into next 4ch sp work * (1–2tr cl, 3ch, 1–2tr cl (for corner) 2ch, 3tr into next 2ch sp, 2ch, rep from * twice, (1–2tr cl, 3ch, 1–2tr cl) into next 4ch sp, 1ch, join to top of 3ch with 1ss.

3rd round   3ch, 1tr into each of next 2tr, 2tr in next sp, into next sp *(2ch, 1–2tr cl, 3ch, 1–2tr cl), 1ch, 2tr in next sp, 1tr into

Plate 1 (*Top left*) The square-motif jacket.

Plate 2 (*Top right*) The Old American or 'Grannie' square and triangle, used to make the jacket in plate 1.

Plate 3 (*Centre left*) The posy square.

Plate 4 (*Centre right*) The roundabout square.

Plate 5 (*Right*) The crossroads square.

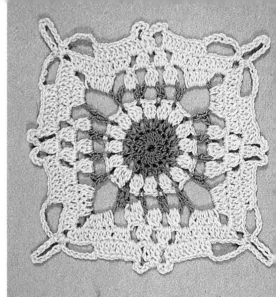

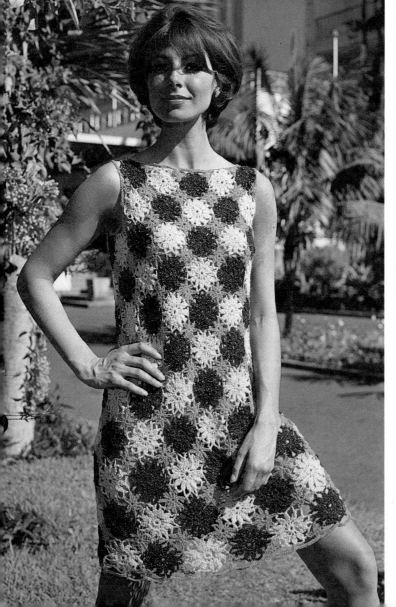

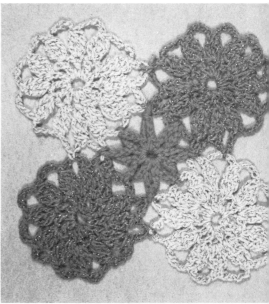

Plate 6 (*Top left*) The cluster motif.

Plate 7 (*Top right*) The two-colour motif.

Plate 8 (*Left*) The circular-motif dress.

Plate 9 (*Above*) Four motifs, as used for the dress in plate 8, joined together.

each of next 3tr, 2tr in sp, rep from * twice, 2ch, (1–2tr cl, 3ch, 1–2tr cl) in next sp, 2ch, 2tr in next sp, join to top of 3ch with 1ss.

4th round   3ch, 1tr in each of next 4tr, 2tr in next sp, * 2ch, (1–2tr cl, 3ch, 1–2tr cl) in next sp, 2ch, 2tr next sp, 1tr in each of next 7tr, 2tr in next sp, Rep from * twice, 2ch, (1–2tr cl, 3ch, 1–2tr cl) into next sp, 2ch, 2tr in next sp, 2tr in next 2tr, join to top of 3ch with 1ss. Fasten off.

CLUSTER MOTIF

Plate 6 shows this motif worked in double-crêpe wool and in Coats No 20 crochet cotton.

Begin with 8ch, join into ring with 1ss.

1st round   24dc into ring, join with 1ss to first dc.

2nd round   4ch, 1–2dbl tr cl in same st, 3ch, (miss 1st, 1–3dbl tr cl in next st, 3ch) 11 times, join to top of first cl with 1ss (12cls).

3rd round   1ss to first sp, into same sp work (4ch, 1–2dbl tr cl, 3ch, 1–3dbl tr cl), * (4ch, 1dc into next sp) twice, 4ch, (1–3dbl tr cl, 3ch, 1–3dbl tr cl) into next sp, rep from * twice, (4ch, 1dc into next sp) twice, 4ch, join to top of first cl with 1ss. Fasten off.

TWO-COLOUR MOTIF

For an illustration of this motif see plate 7.

Using first colour begin with 4ch.

1st round   15tr into ring, join to top of first st with ss.

2nd round   4ch, * 1tr into next tr, 1ch, rep from *, join into 3rd of 4ch with ss. Fasten off.

3rd round   Join in 2nd shade to first sp, 3ch, leaving the last loop of each st on hook, work 2tr into same st, yoh and draw through all loops on hook (1cl made), * 2ch, 3tr cl into next sp, rep from * ending with 2ch, ss into top of first cl. Fasten off.

4th round   Rejoin first colour to first sp, 1dc into same sp, * (5ch 1dc into next sp) 3 times, 10ch, 1dc into next sp, rep from * omit 1dc at end of third repeat, ss into first dc. Fasten off.

5th round   Rejoin 2nd colour to first 5ch loop, 3ch, 2tr cl into same loop, * (3ch, 3tr cl into next loop) twice, 3ch, work into next corner loop (5tr 3ch 5tr,) 3ch, 3tr cl in next loop, rep from * omitting the last 3tr cl, join to top of first cl with ss.

6th round   Ss into first sp, 3ch, 2tr cl into same sp, * 2 ch, 3tr cl into next sp, 2ch, 3tr into next sp, 1tr into each of next 5tr, into next corner sp work (3tr, 3ch, 3tr) 1tr into each of next 5tr, 3tr into next sp, 2ch, 1 3tr cl into next sp, rep from * omitting the last 3tr cl, join to top of first cl with ss.

7th round   Ss to first sp, 3ch, 1 2tr cl into same sp, * 5ch, 3tr into next sp, 1tr into each of next 6tr, 7ch, into corner sp work (1dc 11ch 1dc) 7ch, miss 5tr, 1tr into each of next 6tr, 3tr into next sp, 5ch, 1–3tr cl into next sp, rep from * omitting the last 3tr cl, join to top of first cl with ss. Fasten off.

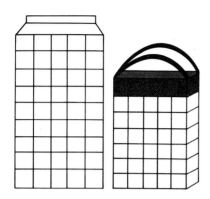

Fig. 3. Positioning the square motifs for the any-length skirt.

Fig. 4. Basic design for the workbag or shopper.

Skirt top

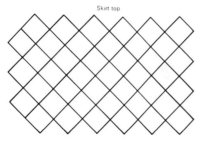

Fig. 5. Positioning the square motifs for the diamond-shaped skirt.

IDEAS FOR FURTHER DESIGNS USING SQUARE MOTIFS
Any-length skirt
Figure 3 shows the simplicity with which a square-motif skirt can be designed and worked in any length. The motifs at the top have to be drawn in to waist size in a series of rows of double crochet or half treble, and an opening at the back allows for a zip fastener or buttons. Finally a pretty edging may be worked round the lower edge.

If the skirt is made with glitter-centred motifs it will grace any evening function.

A workbag or shopper
Figure 4 shows the basic pattern for a bag with a panel of motifs at the base and sides, allowing for plenty of storage space. The top may be finished with several rows of plain crochet, and two handles complete the article.

Alternatively, the bag may be mounted on a pair of wooden handles, with a suitable side division in the plain top to allow for easy access.

Diamond-shaped skirt
A skirt with square motifs set to form a diamond shape looks charming with a plain jumper or jacket top. Figure 5 shows a design in which the side motifs dovetail into each other in the making up.

There is really no end to the possibilities of design in this manner, and it is not confined only to fashion. A tablecloth, bedspread or trolley cloth, all of which are easy to work out, look special in any home.

Circular motifs

Square motifs have recently become very popular, but circular ones are also great favourites with most crocheters although, because of their shape, joining is not quite as simple as it is for their square counterparts.

Round motifs may be used singly for place-mats, doilys and other small items; or one motif may be enlarged so as to form a tablecloth. Joined together, either by crochet stitches as each motif nears completion, or with special 'filler', they can be used to form a great many beautiful things.

The adaptation of the motif to the modern fashion scene has done a great deal towards popularizing the desire among large numbers of people to create attractive, personalized garments which are just a little different from the usual fashion ideas. The square motif seems to pop up everywhere in one form or another, yet comparatively few garments are based on circular shapes. So, let us begin to put this right by working out an attractive dress with a sparkling party air, made entirely of circular shapes of only two rounds each.

This dress should be well within the capabilities of 'girls' of all ages who wish to give a boost to their wardrobe.

The round-motif dress

This dress is illustrated in plate 8.

MEASUREMENTS
Bust 89 cm (35 in.)
Width round lower edge 117 cm (46 in.)
Length from shoulder 79 cm (31 in.)

YARN
The yarn selected for the dress was Lister Bel Air Starspun, which is made of 88 per cent Courtelle with 12 per cent glitter effect. Each ball weighs 25 grammes.

HOOK TEST
Three test motifs were made to the following instructions, the first with a No 3·50 hook, the second with a 3·00 and the third with a 2·50 hook. The result was:

Motif worked with 3·50 hook measured 7·5 cm (3 in.) diameter.
Motif worked with 3·00 hook measured 6·6 cm (2·75 in.) diameter.
Motif worked with 2·50 hook measured 6·0 cm (2·5 in.) diameter.

In order to give a little shaping at the waist, and to obtain the correct length, the lower motifs have to be worked on the largest hook, the 3·50; Nos 3·00 and 2·50 are substituted for the 5th round, and No 2·50 is used for the remainder of the garment.

TO WORK THE MOTIF
With No 3·50 hook, begin with 6ch, join into a ring with 1ss.
1st round Into ring work 4ch (standing as 1tr, 1ch), * 1tr, 1ch, rep from * 10 times, join to 3rd of 4ch with 1ss. (12 spokes.)
2nd round 5ch, * yoh twice, hook into base of 5 starting ch, yoh and pull through, yoh and draw through 2 lps, yoh and draw through 2 lps, rep from * once, yoh and draw through all lps on hook, 6ch, ** (yoh twice, hook into top of next tr, yoh, and draw through, yoh and draw through 2 lps, yoh and draw through 2 lps) three times, working into the top of same tr each time, yoh and draw through all lps on hook, 6ch, rep from ** into each tr, making 12 petals. Join to top of first petal with 1ss. Break off yarn.

YARN REQUIREMENTS

To give the dress an extra special air, it was decided to use two colours for the larger motifs, one half the number to be made in each. A third colour was introduced for the 'filler' flowers to join the motifs.

For the purposes of calculation the larger motif worked on the 3·50 hook was used, the difference in yarn consumption compared with those made on the smaller hooks being minimal.

Weight of 1 motif 1·05 gm
Weight of 3 'fillers' 1·05 gm

Figure 6 shows the dress laid flat for ease of calculation, although actually it is worked in a circular manner from the lower edge, the motifs being joined together as the work progresses (see plate 9). The 'fillers' on the right of the diagram will, of course, be joined to the motifs on the left as each round of motifs is made and joined.

Number of motifs to be made:

9 rounds each of 14	126
2 rows each of 5 (back and front bust)	20
Total	146

Number of fill-in flowers:

8 rounds each of 14	112
4 round each of 5	20
Edgings, equivalent to say 50 fill-ins	50
Total	182

Fig. 6. Calculations and positioning of motifs for the round-motif dress. The illustration shows the dress lying flat although it is actually worked in a circular manner from the lower edge.

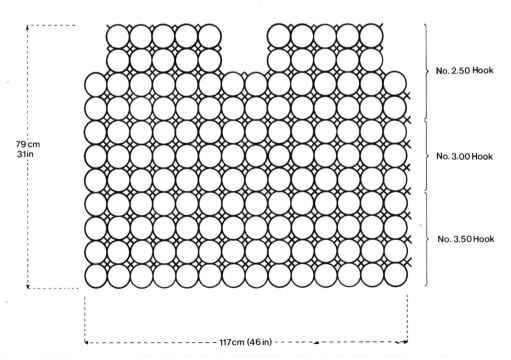

79 cm
31 in

No. 2.50 Hook

No. 3.00 Hook

No. 3.50 Hook

117cm (46 in)

SUMMARY OF YARN REQUIRED

Shade A   half of total 146 motifs,   25-gm balls
     i.e. 73 motifs at 1·05 gm each = 76·65 gm   (say 4 balls)
Shade B   half of total 146 motifs,
     i.e. 73 motifs at 1·05 gm each = 76·65 gm   (say 4 balls)
Shade C   fill-ins at 0·35 gm each =   63·7 gm   (say 3 balls)

TO MAKE THE DRESS

Measurements: as on page 23
Materials: Lister Bel Air Starspun—colour A—4 × 25-gm
           balls; colour B—4 × 25-gm balls; colour
           C—3 × 25-gm balls
Tension: motif on No 3·50 hook 7·5 cm (3 in.) diameter
         motif on No 3·00 hook 7·0 cm (2·75 in.) diameter
         motif on No 2·50 hook 6·5 cm (2·5 in.) diameter
Abbreviations: see full list, page 13

1st row of motifs

Begin at lower edge. Using a No 3·50 hook and colour A, work the first motif as instructed on page 00. Fasten off.

Using colour B, make another motif in the same way, but after 10 petals have been made join to the first motif thus: work * 3ch, hook under a 6ch lp of first motif, yoh and draw through the 6ch lp and st on hook, so making the 4th ch of a 6ch lp, 2ch, work next petal, rep from * once, end with 6ch, ss into top of first petal of motif.

Using A, make another motif similarly, and join to the 2nd motif at 2 sps exactly opposite the first 2, leaving 4 6ch sps on each side of the joins.

Work 14 motifs in alternate colours, joining into a circle on the 14th motif as follows: Work until the first petal has been made, join the next 2 6ch lps to the 13th motif, work 1 petal 1 6ch lp 4 times, then 1 petal, 3ch, and join to the first motif exactly opposite the first 2 lps, leaving 4 sps between the joins.

2nd row of motifs

Placing A over B and B over A, work 10 petals and join to any motif at the 2nd and 3rd 6ch sp.

Next motif

Make a first petal, 3ch, and counting anticlockwise from the last join, join into the 3rd sp, then into the 2nd, work 1 petal, 1 sp, 1 petal, 3ch, and join into 2nd and 3rd sps of next motif of first row, complete the motif.

This will leave a square gap between four motifs, formed by 1 free sp from each motif. These gaps will be filled with a 'fill-in flower' as indicated in Fig. 6.

The fill-in flower

Using colour C and the same size hook as for motifs, work 5ch, join into ring with ss, 4ch, hook through one 6ch space in the square gap between motifs, yoh, and draw through sp and st on hook, 4ch, 1dc under 5ch ring, 4ch, hook through next join of motifs, yoh and draw through lp and st on hook, 4ch, 1dc under 5ch ring. Rep the round working alternately into free lp and join of motifs, making 8 petals.

Note: The hook sizes for motifs and fill-in flowers will have to be changed as follows:

First 4 rounds use No 3·50 hook
Rounds 5 to 7 inclusive use No 3·00 hook
Rounds 8 to top of dress use No 2·50 hook

When the 9th round has been worked, divide for front and back, leaving 2 motifs at each side for the underarms.

Work 2 rows of motifs over each of the 2 sets of 5 motifs for back and front of dress.

Shoulder

With a fill-in flower, join the motif at the outside edge of the front to the opposite outside motif of the back, make 5ch and join into a ring with a ss, * make 4ch, hook under sp opposite the joins at other side, leaving 4 free sps at outside of motif, yoh and draw through sp and st on hook, 4ch, dc into ring, rep from * into next sp, 8ch, 1dc into ring, 8ch, 1dc into ring, * 4ch, hook into sp of motif on other side, yoh, draw through sp and st on hook, 4ch, 1dc into ring, rep from * into next sp 8ch, 1dc into ring, 8ch, 1dc into ring. (8 petals made.) Join the other shoulder similarly.

Edge spaces

Work 3 petals of flower in spaces between motifs across the neck, round armholes and along hemline. Make 5ch and join into ring with ss, 4ch, hook under sp next to join of motifs, yoh, and pull through sp and st on hook, 4ch, 1dc into ring, 4ch, hook into join of motifs, yoh and draw through join and st on hook, 4ch, 1dc into ring, 4ch, hook into next sp, yoh, draw through sp and st on hook, 4ch, 1dc into ring. (3 petals made.)

Neck edge

Using C and starting from the small motif at shoulder, 1dc into first loose petal, 4ch, 1dc into next loose petal, 6ch, 1dc into centre petal of large motif, * 7ch, 1dc into centre ring of 3-petal flower, 7ch, 1dc into centre of larger motif, rep from * to last large motif, and work the other side similarly, 1ss into first dc of round.
Next round Work 6dc under each 7ch lp and 3dc under each 4ch lp, and 1dc over each dc of previous row. Break off yarn.

Armholes
Work in the same way.

Hem
Using No 2·50 hook and C work 7ch between top petal of larger motif and the ring of 3-petal flower, working 1dc into each petal of the large motif and ring of small motif as they appear. On next round work 6dc under each 7ch lp and 1dc over each dc of previous row.

Note: There will be some yarn of each olour remaining after the dress is completed. Why not design and make a matching headscarf, or stole, or perhaps a small clutch bag to add the finishing touch to a very pretty garment?

The panelled maxi-dress

This glamorous full-length dress, illustrated in plate 10, would be a source of admiration at any social function. It is designed in a completely different way from the small-motif type, having six long panels, worked in a scallop-shell pattern from the top to lower edge. This gives an unusual hemline, at the same time providing a neat square neck.

The length of the dress can be adapted as desired, and the fringes can be omitted or replaced by additional rows of crochet. Each panel is edged and joined to its neighbour; the neckline is formed by placing the panels as shown in Fig. 7.

Shaping is ingeniously contrived by the skilful manoeuvring of different sized hooks, thus obviating increasing and decreasing as work progresses.

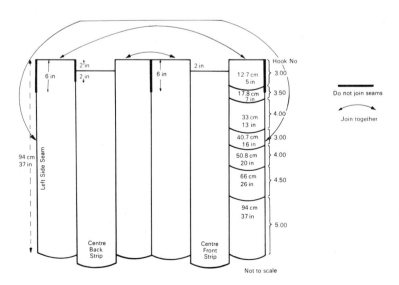

Fig. 7. Positioning the panels for the maxi-dress.

MEASUREMENTS
Bust 86 cm (34 in.)
Hips 91 cm (36 in.)
Length from shoulder 109·5 cm (43 in.) exluding fringes

Note: Larger sizes can quite successfully be made by using larger hooks.

YARN
Lee Target Duo double-crêpe Tricel with nylon.

HOOK TEST
One panel was worked according to the pattern, beginning with a No 3·00 hook for the first ten rows. This was followed by ten rows each with No 3·50, 4·00, 4·50 and 5·00. Each row on which the hook was changed was marked with a small safety pin. The result was:

With No 3·00 hook, width = 10·8 cm (4·25 in.).
With No 3·50 hook, width = 11·5 cm (4·5 in.).
With No 4·00 hook, width = 12·2 cm (4·75 in.).
With No 4·50 hook, width = 12·9 cm (5 in.).
With No 5·00 hook, width = 13·5 cm (5·25 in.).

It was decided to use the hooks in the order indicated in Fig. 7, thus giving extra width over bust, less over waist, more at hips and still more at lower edge.

Note: Every experienced crocheter appreciates the importance of working to correct tension. In this case it is vital, as too much width could turn a lovely gown into a sack, and too little would reveal far too much body shape.

SUMMARY OF YARN REQUIRED
One whole panel was worked, using the hooks indicated in Fig. 7 and including the edging, according to instructions on page 29. The panel consumed 3·25 balls.

Amount required for 6 panels is
   6 × 3·25   = 19·5 balls
Amount required for fringes   = 2   balls

                Total yarn requirment   21·5 balls (say 22 balls)

TO MAKE THE PANEL DRESS
Measurements: as above
Materials: Lee Target Duo double-crêpe Tricel with nylon
22 × 25-gm balls
Tension: as above
Abbreviations: see page 13.

The basic strip (see Fig. 8)
Note: The turning ch counts as 1tr.

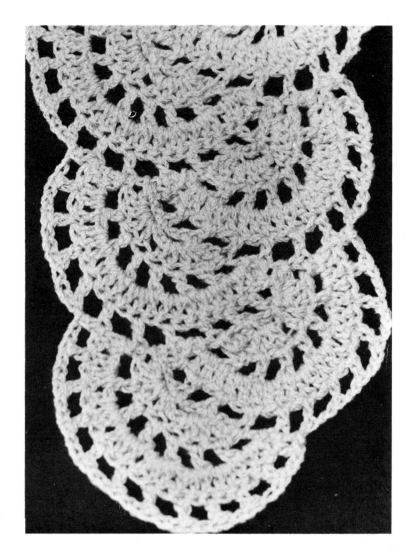

Fig. 8. The scallop-shell pattern for
the basic strip of the maxi-dress.

Begin with 28ch.

1st row 1dc into 8th ch from hook, 3ch, miss 3ch, 1dc into next ch, 2ch, turn.

2nd row 4tr into next sp, 1tr into next dc, 4tr into next sp, 3ch, turn.

3rd row 1tr into next tr, (2ch, miss 1tr, 1tr into next tr) 4 times, 2ch, 1tr into last dc worked on first row, miss 2 foundation ch, ss into next foundation ch, 1ch, miss 1 foundation ch, ss into next foundation ch, turn.

4th row (1tr into next tr, 2tr into next sp) 5 times, 1tr into next tr, 1tr into last sp, 3ch, turn.

5th row (1tr into next tr, 1ch, miss 1tr) 5 times, (1tr into next tr, 2ch, miss 1tr) 3 times, 1tr into next tr, miss 2 foundation ch, ss into next foundation ch, 3ch, turn.

6th row (Miss next sp, 1dc into next tr, 3ch) twice, miss next sp, 1dc into next tr, turn.

7th row Miss next sp, 1tr into next dc, 2tr into next sp, 1tr into next dc, 3tr into next sp, miss 1 foundation ch, ss into next foundation ch, 2ch, miss 1 foundation ch, ss into next foundation ch, 2ch, turn.

8th row Miss next tr, (1tr, into next tr, 2ch) 6 times, ss into next sp on previous motif, 1ch, ss into next tr on previous motif, turn.

9th row (2tr into next sp, 1tr into next tr) 7 times, miss 1 foundation ch, ss into next foundation ch, 2ch, miss 1 foundation ch, ss into last foundation ch, 2ch, turn.

10th row (Miss 1tr, 1tr into next tr, 3ch) 3 times, (miss 1tr, 1tr into next tr, 2ch) 7 times, miss 1tr, 1tr into next tr, ss into next sp on previous motif, 3ch, turn.

11th row (Miss next sp, 1dc into next tr, 3ch) twice, miss next sp, 1dc into next tr, turn.

12th row Miss next sp, 1tr into next dc, 2tr into next sp, 1tr into next dc, 3tr into next sp, ss to next sp on previous motif, 1ch, ss to next sp on previous motif, 2ch, turn.

13th row Miss next tr, (1tr into next tr, 2ch) 6 times, ss into next sp on previous motif, 1ch, ss into next tr on previous motif, turn.

14th row (2tr into next sp, 1tr into next tr) 7 times, ss into next sp on previous motif, 1ch, ss to last sp on previous motif, 2ch, turn.

15th row (Miss 1tr, 1tr into next tr, 3ch) 3 times, (miss 1tr, 1tr into next tr, 2ch) 7 times, miss 1tr, 1tr into next tr, ss into next sp on previous motif, 3ch, turn.

16th row (Miss next sp, 1dc into next tr, 3ch) twice, miss next sp, 1dc into next tr, turn.

17th row Miss next sp, 1tr into next dc, 2tr into next sp, 1tr into next dc, 3tr into next sp, ss to next tr on previous motif, 1ch, ss to next sp on previous motif, 2ch, turn.

18th row Miss next tr, (1tr into next tr, 2ch) 6 times, ss to next sp on previous motif, 1ch, ss into next tr on previous motif, turn.

19th row (2tr into next sp, 1tr into next tr) 7 times, ss into next tr on previous motif, 1ch, ss into next sp on previous motif, 2ch, turn.

Rows 15 to 19 inclusive form the pattern.

Side strips (4)
Reference to Fig. 7 will reveal that 4 side strips are required as follows:

The measurements are taken to top of last motif worked.

Using 3·00 hook, begin basic strip and work in pattern until work measures 12·7 cm (5 in.).

Change to 3·50 hook and continue in pattern until work measures 17·8 cm (7 in.) from beginning.

Change to 4·00 hook and continue in pattern until work measures 33 cm (13 in.) from beginning.

Change to 3·00 hook, and continue in pattern until work measures 40·7 cm (16 in.) from beginning.

Change to 4·00 hook and continue in pattern until work measures 50·8 cm (20 in.) from beginning.

Change to 4·50 hook and continue in pattern until work measures 66 cm (26 in.) from beginning.

Change to 5·00 hook and continue in pattern until work measures 94 cm (37 in.) from beginning, completing last motif.

Note: All 4 strips ending with the same motif. Fasten off.

Strips for centre back and front (2)

Using 3·00 hook, begin basic strip and work in pattern until work measures 7·6 cm (3 in.) from beginning.

Change to 3·50 hook and continue in pattern until work measures 12·7 cm (5 in.) from beginning.

Change to 4·00 hook, and continue in pattern until work measures 27·9 cm (11 in.) from beginning.

Change to 3·00 hook and continue in pattern until work measures 35·5 cm (14 in.) from beginning.

Change to 4·00 hook and continue in pattern until work measures 45·7 cm (18 in.) from beginning.

Change to 4·50 hook and continue in pattern until work measures 61 cm (24 in.) from beginning.

Change to 5·00 hook and continue in pattern until the same number of motifs have been worked as on side strips. Fasten off.

Edging for side strips

This is for working down the side edges of the strips only. Place a pin 15·2 cm (12 in.) down from beginning edge (shoulder). Rejoin yarn and, using 3·50 hook with right side of work facing, work in dc along edge as far as pin position; now place pin 38·1 cm (15 in.) down from shoulder seam, and work in tr as far as this pin; now work in dtr down to lower edge (do not turn corners of last motifs, but end on straight edges). Beginning at lower edge with right side facing, work up the other side of strip to correspond (this time changing from dtr to tr to dc).

Edging for centre back and front strips

Place pin 10·2 cm (4 in.) down from beginning edge, and next pin 38·1 cm (15 in.) down from beginning edge, then work as given for edging for side strips, changing stitch as pin positions are reached, working 5 cm (2 in.) of dtr less than side strips at lower edge.

TO MAKE UP

Join as indicated in Fig. 7. Join shoulder and left side seam as indicated by arrows. Lightly press all seams.

The six-hour waistcoat

This waistcoat, shown in plate 11, is simple in style and pattern so it is a useful design from which to learn the technique of working rows to a particular pattern.

In triple-thick yarn, it can be crocheted and worn within six hours by someone who wields the hook at an average speed. It is lacey in appearance, economical in yarn consumption, and will give warmth over back and shoulders without the bulk of sleeves. For wear over a dress, a skirt, or slacks, it can be made any length.

MEASUREMENTS
Bust 86·00 cm (34–36 in.)
Length from top of shoulder 63·5 cm (25 in.)

YARN
Lee Target Aran Wool in 50-gm balls.

CHOOSING THE STITCH PATTERN
The old saying 'more holes, less yarn' is very true of this garment, and it has been proved so often that closely woven material does not necessarily provide more body warmth than the more open type.

In this 8-row pattern, see Fig. 9, the main feature is the two rows of 6-treble shells, the first row worked in complete shells, the second beginning and ending with one half-shell and having one whole shell less along the row. The shell rows are divided by one row of 1-chain spaces, 1 row of trebles and another space row.

TENSION TEST
Using a No 5·00 hook and working over 30 trebles for 8 rows
7tr = 5 cm (2 in.)
2 rows = 2·5 cm (1 in.)

Fig. 9. The 8-row pattern for the six-hour waistcoat.

PLANNING THE WAISTCOAT

Style
Low V-neck. The shaping at fronts begins on the 33rd row, and is reduced gradually by 2 shells to 3 at the top.

Armhole decreases of 7 stitches each (1 shell) begin on the 39th row.

Fastenings   5 crocheted buttons with corresponding chain buttonholes. If preferred, the waistcoat may be made without any fastenings.

Edgings   2 rows of dc round each armhole and 3 rows of dc round waistcoat edges.

Number of stitches to begin the back   The width of the back is 45·5 cm (18 in.). At 7 trebles per 5 cm (2 in.), plus 2 stitches for movement and 1 turning chain, the number of stitches required will be:
$(7 \times 9) + 2 + 1 = 66$ch
First row = 65tr
This will allow the formation of 11 shells on the first shell row.

Number of stitches to begin each front   Allow 3 more stitches for each front than one-half total of back, i.e. 36 chain
First row = 35tr
This will allow 6 shells on the first shell row.

THE 1-PIECE YARN TEST
With a No 5·00 hook, one side of the front was worked in the pattern selected. This took exactly 1·5 balls. Both fronts, therefore, will together require 3 balls. The back, although slightly narrower than both fronts together, is worked right up to the back of the neck and will also take 3 balls. The edgings will require 1 ball.

The total amount of yarn needed will, therefore, be 7 balls.

TO MAKE THE WAISTCOAT
Materials: 7 × 50-gm balls of Lee Target Aran wool;
No 5·00 crochet hook for main body of waistcoat;
No 4·50 crochet hook for armbands and edgings;
No 3·50 crochet hook for buttons; 5 button moulds (optional).
Abbreviations: see page 13.

The Back
Using No 5·00 hook, begin with 66ch.
1st row   1tr into 3rd ch from hook, 1tr into each rem ch, 3ch, turn, (2 of these ch represent first tr of next row), 65tr.
2nd row   Miss first tr, * miss next tr, 1tr into next tr, 1ch, rep from * to last 2tr, miss next tr, 1tr into next tr, *no* ch, turn.

3rd row   1dc into first tr, 4ch, * miss 2 one ch sps, 1dc into next 1ch sp, 5ch, rep from * to last two 1ch sps, 4ch instead of 5ch on last rep, 1dc into 2nd ch of turning ch, 2ch, turn.

4th row   5tr into 4ch sp, * 1dc into dc of previous row, 6tr into 5ch sp, rep from * to end 4ch sp, 1dc into dc of previous row, 5tr into this sp, 1tr into end dc, *no* ch, turn.

5th row   1dc into first tr, 2ch, miss 2tr, 1dc into next tr, * 5ch, 1dc into 3rd tr of next shell, rep from * to last shell, 2ch, 1dc into top of turning ch, 2ch, turn.

6th row   2tr into 2ch sp, * 1dc into dc of previous row, 6tr into 5ch sp, rep from * to last 2ch sp, 1dc into dc of previous row, 2tr into 2ch sp, 1tr into end dc, *no* ch, turn.

7th row   1dc into first tr, 4ch, * 1dc into 3rd tr of next sh, 5ch, rep from * to last shell, working 4ch instead of 5ch on last rep, 1dc into top of turning ch, 3ch, turn.

8th row   Miss first dc and first ch, 1tr into next ch, * miss 1ch, 1ch, 1tr into next ch, miss 1dc, 1ch, 1tr into next ch, 1ch, miss 1ch, 1tr into next ch, rep from * to end dc, 1ch, 1tr into end dc (32 1ch sps), 2ch, turn.

9th row   Miss first tr,* 1tr into next ch, 1tr into next tr, rep from * to end 3ch, 1tr into top ch, 1tr into 2nd ch, 3ch, turn (65 trs).

Rep 2nd to 9th rows (inclusive) 3 times, then 2nd to 6th rows (inclusive) once, no ch, turn.

Shape armholes

1st row   Ss over 7sts, 1dc into next tr, 4ch, * 1dc into 3rd tr of next shell, 5ch, rep from * to last complete shell, working 4ch on last rep, 1dc into 3rd tr of this shell, 3ch, turn.

Rep 8th and 9th rows of patt once, then 2nd to 9th rows and 2nd row once then 9th row once more. Fasten off.

Left front

Using No 5·00 hook, make 36ch.

Work 1st to 9th rows of patt as given for back once, 2nd to 9th rows twice, then 2nd to 8th rows once, 2ch, turn after last row.

Shape front

1st row   Miss first tr, * 1tr into next ch, 1tr into next tr, rep from * to last 2tr, make dec in last 2tr thus: (yoh, insert hook into next tr, and draw up a loop, yoh, and draw through 2 loops) twice, yoh, and draw wool through rem 3 loops, 3ch, turn.

2nd row   Miss first 2tr, * 1tr into next tr, 1ch, miss 1tr, rep from * to last tr, 1tr into end tr.

3rd row   1dc into first tr, 4ch, * miss two 1ch spaces, 1dc into next 1ch space, 5ch, rep from * to last 1ch space, working 2ch on last rep, 1dc into top of turning ch, no ch, turn.

4th row   2tr into 2ch sp, * 1dc into dc of previous row, 6tr into 5ch sp, rep from * to 4ch space, 1dc into dc of previous row, 5tr into 4ch space, 1tr into end dc, no ch, turn.

5th row   1dc into first tr, 2ch, * 1dc into 3rd tr of shell, 5ch, rep from * to last half shell working 2ch on last rep, 1dc into end tr, 2ch, turn.

6th row   2tr into first 2ch space, * 1dc into dc of previous row, 6tr into 5ch space, rep from * to 2ch sp, 1dc into dc of previous row, 2tr into 2ch space, 1tr into end dc, no ch, turn.

Shape armhole

7th row   Ss over 7sts, 1dc into next tr, 4ch, * 1dc into 3rd tr of next shell, 5ch, rep from * to last half shell, working 4ch instead of 5ch on last rep, 1dc into end tr, 3ch, turn.

8th row   Miss first dc and ch, 1tr into next ch, * miss 1ch, 1ch, 1tr into next ch, miss 1dc, 1ch, 1tr into next ch, miss 1ch, 1ch, 1tr into next ch, rep from * to end dc, 1ch, 1tr into this dc, 2ch, turn.

Rep 1st to 6th row of shaping once.

Next row   1dc into next tr, 4ch, * 1dc into 3rd tr of next shell, 5ch, rep from * to last half shell, working 4ch instead of 5 on last rep, 1dc into end tr, 3ch, turn.

Rep 8th row, then 1st and 2nd rows of shaping, 2ch, turn.

Last row * 1tr into next ch, 1tr into next tr, rep from * to end. Fasten off.

Right front

Work exactly as left front to front shaping.

Shape front

1st row   Miss first tr, make dec in next 2sts as before, * 1tr into next ch, 1tr into next tr, rep from * to turning 3ch, 1tr into top ch, 1tr into 2nd ch, 3ch, turn.

2nd row   Miss first tr, * miss next tr, 1ch, 1tr into next tr, rep from * to last 3tr, miss next 2tr, 1ch, 1tr into top of turning ch.

3rd row   1dc into first tr, miss 1ch sp, 2ch, * 1dc into next 1ch space, 5ch, miss two 1ch spaces, rep from * to last three 1ch spaces, 1dc into next 1ch space, 4ch, 1dc into top of turning ch, 2ch, turn.

4th row   5tr into 4ch space, * 1dc into dc of previous row, 6tr into next 5ch space, rep from * to end 2ch space, 1dc into dc of previous row, 1tr into this space, 1tr into end dc.

5th row   1dc into first tr, 2ch, * 1dc into 3rd tr of next shell, 5ch, rep from * to last shell, 2ch, 1dc into top of turning ch, 2ch, turn.

6th row   2tr into 2ch space, * 1dc into dc of previous row, 6tr into 5ch space, rep from * to last 2ch space, 1dc into dc of previous row, 2tr into 2ch space, 1tr into end dc, no ch, turn.

Shape armhole

7th row   1dc into first tr, 4ch, * 1dc into 3rd tr of next shell, 5ch, rep from * to last complete shell, work 4ch instead of 5ch on last rep, 1dc into 3rd tr of this shell, 3ch, turn.

35

8th row Miss first dc and ch, 1tr into next ch, * miss next ch, 1ch, 1tr into next ch, miss dc, 1ch, 1tr into next ch, miss next ch, 1ch, 1tr into next ch, rep from * to last dc, 1ch, 1tr into end dc, 2ch, turn.

Rep 1st, 2nd, 3rd, 4th, 5th and 6th rows of shaping.

Next row 1dc into first tr, 4ch, * 1dc into 3rd tr of next shell, 5ch, rep from * to last half shell, work 4ch instead of 5ch on last rep, 1dc into end tr, 3ch, turn.

Rep 8th row, then 1st and 2nd rows of shaping, 2ch, turn.

Last row * 1tr into next ch, 1tr into next tr, rep from * to end. Fasten off.

Armbands

Press each piece carefully. Sew up shoulder and side seams. With No 4·50 hook work 2 rows of dc evenly round each armhole. Fasten off.

Front edging

Using No 4·50 hook, work 3 rows of dc evenly up right front, across back neck, down left front, working 5 button loops on 3rd row evenly up right front thus: 1dc into next dc, 5ch, miss 2dc, 1dc into next dc.

Buttons

If using button moulds, make crochet covers as follows: Using No 3·50 hook, make 4ch, join into a ring with 1ss.

1st round   8dc into ring, join with 1ss, 1ch,

2nd round   1dc into each dc of previous round.

3rd round   1dc into each dc of previous round.

4th round   1dc into every 3rd dc of previous round.

Thread sewing needle and run round top of last round, draw up over mould. If no mould is available, fill the centre with the same wool and draw thread up over filling. Make 4 more buttons similarly.

Press all seams. Sew on buttons to correspond with the loops.

Mother's and daughter's dresses

These dresses (plate 12) in exactly the same style, one for mother and one for daughter, provide a good basic guide from which the designer may work.

The simple one-row mini-shell stitch (see Fig. 10) in which the dresses are made eases the task of working out a more complex pattern. All kinds of alternatives in style, shape and size will, no doubt, be evolved as a result of the guidance given here.

4-ply yarn is recommended for these garments; it takes a little longer to make up but you will find that you use less yarn, and the dresses drop less than they would if they were made with a heavier thread.

MEASUREMENTS

	Child	Mother
Chest/bust	61 cm (24 in.)	91·5 cm (36 in.)
Length from shoulder	43 cm (17 in.)	83·75 cm (33 in.)
Allowance for possible drop	2·5 cm (1 in.)	5 cm (2 in.)
Undersleeve seam	6·25 cm (2·5 in.)	14 cm (5·5 in.)

YARN
Lister Lavenda 4-ply wool.

STITCH PATTERN
(1tr 2ch 1dc—1 shell) in each st.

HOOK TEST
Using a No 4·00 hook and working over 20 shells and 15 rows
$7\frac{1}{2}$ shells = 10 cm (4 in.) wide
7 rows = 5 cm (2 in.) deep

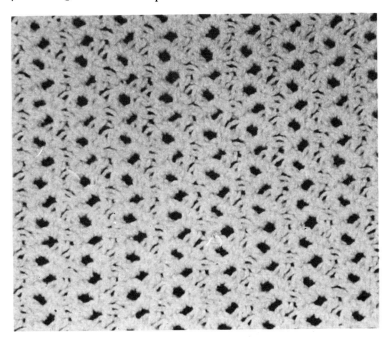

Fig. 10. The 1-row mini-shell pattern for the mother's and daughter's dresses.

PLANNING THE GARMENTS
Each dress is worked upwards from the hemline. The skirts are slightly shaped at the sides by a series of decreases (see Fig. 11). Striped contrast is provided in the back and front yokes, round sleeves and neck, by alternate rows of contrast colour.

A back neck opening gives ample room for easy access, and the short sleeves give extra warmth over the shoulders and upper arms, without the bulk of longer sleeves.

WORKING DETAILS
A No 4·00 hook is used for the main parts of both dresses, and a

37

No 3·00 hook for neck and sleeve edges.

	Daughter	Mother
Hemline begins with	28 shells	40 shells
Hemline width	37·5 cm (15 in.)	56 cm (22 in.)
Both front and back skirt	22 shells	34 shells
decrease at side to width of	30·0 cm (12 in.)	46·0 cm (18 in.)
Both armholes decrease	20 shells	30 shells
one shell each side to		(2 each side)
Contrast stripes front and	9 each	11 each
back yoke		
Contrast stripes each sleeve	2	4
Back opening, buttons	2	4
Back opening, buttonholes	2	4
Back opening begins after	2nd stripe	3rd stripe
Front neck width	11 cm (4·5 in.)	15 cm (6 in.)
Front neck depth	3·25 cm (1·25 in.)	4 cm (1·5 in.)
Front neck shaping begins		
after	7th stripe	8th stripe
Front neck, leave centre	6 shells	10 shells

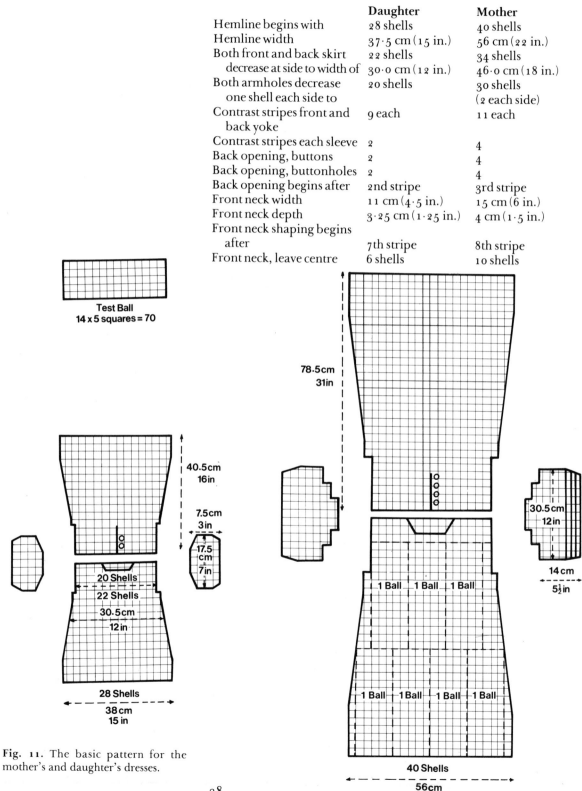

Test Ball
14 x 5 squares = 70

40.5cm
16in

7.5cm
3in

17.5
cm
7in

20 Shells

22 Shells

30.5cm

12in

28 Shells

38cm
15in

78·5cm
31in

1 Ball 1 Ball 1 Ball

1 Ball 1 Ball 1 Ball 1 Ball

40 Shells

56cm
22in

30.5cm
12in

14cm
5½in

Fig. 11. The basic pattern for the mother's and daughter's dresses.

TEST FOR YARN REQUIREMENT
Work a test with 1 ball over 26 shells.
Measurement = 35·5 cm (14 in.) × 12·5 cm (5 in.)
Number of shells worked = 442
Number of squares worked = 70
Main colour—estimated requirement:

	Daughter	Mother
Total number of squares in whole dress	447	1,338
Number of balls required	$447 \div 70 = 6 \cdot 3$	$1{,}338 \div 70 = 19$

Contrast colour—estimated requirement:

	Daughter	Mother
Approx number of shells in whole dress (contrast)	386	762
Number of balls required	$386 \div 442 = 0 \cdot 8$	$762 \div 442 = 1 \cdot 7$

SUMMARY OF YARN REQUIRED
The estimated amount of contrasting yarn must now be subtracted from the estimated amount of main colour yarn:

	Daughter	Mother
Main colour	$6 \cdot 3 - 0 \cdot 8 = 5 \cdot 5$	$19 - 1 \cdot 7 = 17 \cdot 3$
To nearest ball	6	18
Contrast (to nearest ball)	1	2

TO MAKE THE DRESSES
Note: Instructions for daughter's dress are printed first; special instructions for mother's dress appear in brackets.
Measurements: as on page 37
Materials: Lister Lavenda 4-ply crêpe wool

	Daughter	Mother
Main colour	6 balls	18 balls
Contrast	1 ball	2 balls
Buttons	2	4

For both dresses use crochet hook No 4·00 for the main body of the garment and No 3·00 for neck and sleeve edges.
Tension: see page 37
Abbreviations: see page 13

The back
Using No 4·00 hook and M wool make 86 (122)ch.
1st row 1dc into 4th ch from hook, miss 2ch, (1tr, 2ch, 1dc) in next ch (shell made), * miss 2ch, 1 shell in next ch, rep from * to end; 3ch, turn (this represents 1tr and 2ch of first shell of next row). (28 and 40 shells, respectively.)
2nd row 1dc in centre sp of first sh, * 1 sh in centre sp of next

sh, rep from * to end, 3ch, turn. (Always turn with 3ch unless otherwise stated.) This second row forms the pattern.

Work 10 (21) rows in pattern, no turning ch after last row. Now proceed as follows:

** **1st row**   1dc in first sh, pattern to last sh, 1dc in this sh, no ch, turn.

2nd row   1 sh is first sh, * 1 sh in next sh, rep from * to end, working last dc on first dc of previous row, 3ch, turn.

3rd row   1dc in first sh, pattern to end.

Work 10 (23) rows in pattern without shaping.**

Repeat from ** to ** once, then 1st to 3rd rows (inclusive) once. 22 (34) shs.

Continue in pattern without further shaping until work measures 29 cm/11·5 in. (60·5 cm/24 in.) from beginning (or desired length to underarm).

Shape armholes

1st row   3 (6) ss across first 1 (2) shs, 3ch, 1dc in next sh, patt to last 1 (2) shs. 20 (30) shs.

Yoke

Do not break off M colour. Draw contrast yarn through M yarn loop, turn.

1st row   3ch (this represents first tr and 2ch), 1dc in first sh, 1 sh in each following sh to end. Do not turn work, leave C loop, return to other side and M yarn.

2nd row   Insert hook in 3ch of previous row, draw M yarn through, make 3ch, 1dc in first sh, 1 sh in each sh to end, drawing C loop left at this side through last dc instead of M yarn, turn, leaving M yarn.

3rd row   Using C yarn, rep 1st row. Do not turn work.

For mother's dress only work 4 more rows in 2-colour pattern, as above.

Do not break off C yarn.

Divide for back opening

Next row   Using M yarn, pattern across 10 (15) shs, do not break off M yarn, draw 2nd ball of C yarn through M loop, 3ch, turn.

Next row   1dc in first sh, patt to end.

Continue in this manner, working alternate rows of M and C until armhole measures 10 cm/4 in. (18 cm/7 in.) from beginning, ending with M row. Fasten off.

1st row   Using M yarn, join with 3ch to first sh of other side at centre, 1dc in this sh, patt to end, drawing C loop left at this side through last dc, 3ch, turn.

2nd row   Using C patt to end, do not turn work, return to M yarn at other side and complete to correspond with first side.

Front

Work exactly as for back, including armhole shaping.

40

Begin 2-colour patt for yoke and work in alternate rows of M and C until work measures 4 (6) rows less than back, to shoulder.

Shape neck
1st row Patt across 7 (10) shs, do not turn work, leave C loop.
2nd row Using M, patt to last sh, 1dc in this sh, drawing C yarn through this dc, 3ch, turn.
3rd row 1dc in first sh, patt to end, do not turn work.
4th row Draw M shade through first dc of previous row, 2ch, 1sh in first sh, patt to end.
Fasten off for the daughter's dress.
For mother's dress continue. Draw C loop through dc at end of 4th row, turn.
5th row Patt to last sh, 1dc in this sh, do not turn work, leave C loop.
6th row Patt to end. Fasten off both yarns.

Both sizes
Miss centre 6 (10) shs, join C yarn with 3ch to dc of next sh, 1dc in centre of sh, patt to end. Do not turn work, leave C loop.
2nd row Join M yarn with 2ch to centre of first sh of previous row, 1 sh in next sh, patt to end, draw C yarn through, 3ch, turn.
3rd row Patt to last sh, 1dc in this sh, do not turn work, leave C loop.
4th row Patt to last sh, 1 sh in this sh, drawing C loop through dc, no ch.
This completes the daughter's. Fasten off both yarns.
For mother's dress continue:
5th row 1dc in first sh, patt to end, do not turn work.
6th row Draw M yarn through 3rd ch of first sh, 3ch, 1dc in this sh, patt to end. Fasten off both yarns.

The sleeves
Using No 3·00 hook and M shade begin with 41 (71) ch, and work 1st row in patt as given for back. 13 (23) shs. Join in C yarn and work 3 (5) more rows in 2-colour patt as given for yoke. Fasten off C.
Do not turn work, using No 4·00 hook continue in patt in M shade only until work measures 7·5 cm/3in. (14 cm/5·5 in.) from beginning, no ch to turn after last row.
Next row 9ss across 3 shs, patt to last 3 shs. No ch. Fasten off daughter's dress yarn.
Mother's dress Rep last row once. Fasten off.

TO MAKE UP
Using a damp cloth and warm iron (for wool), press each piece carefully on the wrong side.
   Sew up shoulder seams. Sew in sleeves, placing last 1·25 cm/0·5 in. (2·5 cm/1 in.) worked to slip stitches at un-

derarm. Sew up side and sleeve seams.

Using No 3·00 hook and M yarn, work 2 rows dc evenly along left side of back opening to form underflap. Work 2 rows dc to correspond along right side of back opening, making 2 (4) buttonholes, evenly spaced, on 2nd row.

To make a buttonhole
Work in dc to buttonhole position, 2ch, miss 2dc, work dc to next position.

Neck edging
With right side facing, using No 3·00 hook, beginning at left side of back opening work 1 row of dc evenly around neck, edge. Fasten off.

Using C yarn with right side facing, beginning at right side of back opening, work dc backwards from left to right as follows: insert hook in last dc of previous row, 1dc in this dc, * 1dc in next dc to right, rep from * to end. Fasten off.

Work edging around sleeves similarly.

Sew on buttons to correspond with buttonholes. Press all seams.

The cardigan-skirt suit

A cardigan suit is useful for all-round-the-year wear. This one, designed in a lacey pattern, can easily be adapted to suit any figure or style (see plate 13). The skirt can be made any length, or extended upwards to form a dress; the three-quarter length sleeves can be widened, lengthened or shortened as desired, or they can be set into a dress instead of the cardigan. The neckline can be changed to V-shape or square, and, by adapting the fronts to match the back, a jumper or pullover can be made.

The buttons, designed to be made in the same yarn as the suit, could be made in a toning shade. Alternatively, manufactured buttons can be attached to the jacket.

It will be seen from Fig. 12 that the cardigan consists of five pieces and the skirt of two. Each piece is worked from the lower edge upwards. The cardigan has a high, round neck and four-button front; each front has a 4-treble border down the front edge.

Shaping is necessary to reduce the width of the back and fronts of the jacket by about 2·5 cm (1 in.) at the armholes. Sleeve shaping is done by beginning at the lower edge with a No 4·00 hook, changing to a 4·50 and finally, nearer the top, to a 5·00 A few stitches are added to each side of the sleeve, within a few rows of the top.

The skirt shaping is done in a similar manner to that of the sleeves, but in reverse, i.e. beginning with the largest size hook, followed in turn by the other two. Edgings are worked in a

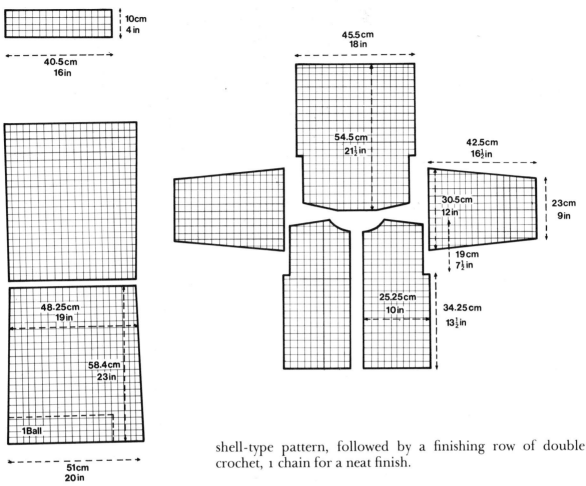

Fig. 12. The basic pattern for the cardigan—skirt suit.

shell-type pattern, followed by a finishing row of double
crochet, 1 chain for a neat finish.

MEASUREMENTS

The jacket
Bust 86–91 cm (34–36 in.)
Length from shoulder 57 cm (22·5 in.)
Undersleeve seam 42 cm (16·5 in.)

The skirt
Hips 91–94 cm (36–37 in.)
Length from waist 61 cm (24 in.)

YARN
Lister 2-spun double-crêpe Tricel-with-nylon yarn. This has a
slight sheen and looks and wears extremely well.

STITCH PATTERN
This is a 6-row lacey pattern which is particularly attractive
when worn over a contrasting coloured foundation (see Fig. 13).

HOOK TEST
A small test piece was worked over 44 stitches and 24 rows, to

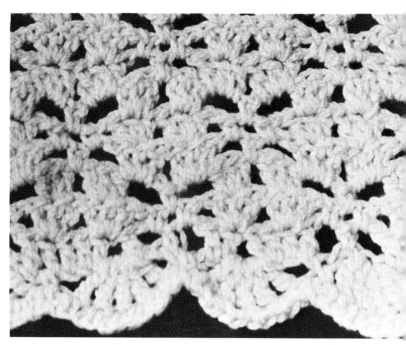

Fig. 13. The 6-row lacey pattern for the cardigan—skirt suit.

the instructions given on page 45 and using No 4·00 hook. A second test on No 4·50 and a third on No 5·00 were also made; each hook produced a satisfactory result.

It was decided to use No 4·50 hook for the main body of the suit and 4·00 and 5·00 for the sleeve and skirt graduations.

TENSION
On No 4·50 hook 1 patt = 6·3 cm (2·5 in.)
6 rows = 5·7 cm (2·25 in.)

WORKING DETAILS
The back
Number of stitches to begin with for correct width—7 patts each of 11sts = 77sts
Number of rows for length of 54·5 cm (21·5 in.) = 60 rows

The fronts
Number of stitches to begin with for correct width—4 patts each of 11sts + 1 = 45sts
Number of rows for length (as back) = 60 rows

The sleeves
Number of sts required to begin = 55sts
Number of sts after increasing 3sts each side at top = 61sts
Number of rows to top (approx) = 44 rows

The skirt
Number of sts required for lower width of 51 cm (20 in.) each piece (back and front)—8 patts each of 11sts = 88sts
Number of rows to top (approx) = 64 rows

TEST FOR YARN REQUIREMENT

To prove the accuracy of the guess test, this method and the graph comparison test are both given for the suit.

Test piece for yarn requirement

1 ball, worked in pattern over 77 stitches ran out at the end of the 11th row. Measurement 40·5 × 10 cm (16 × 4 in.)

Guess test

For its 60 rows the back will consume	5·5 balls
Back and front of skirt will use approx 1 ball each more than back	13·0 balls
Both fronts of jacket will use approx 0·5 ball more than back	6·0 balls
Both sleeves will use same as back plus 0·5 ball	6·0 balls
Edgings and buttons	1·0 ball
Total	31·5 balls
To nearest ball	32·0 balls

Graph comparison test

Total number of squares covered by whole design	2,013
Total number of squares covered by test	64
Number of balls required for suit (2,013 ÷ 64)	31·4 balls
To nearest ball	32·0 balls

TO MAKE THE SUIT

Measurements: as on page 43
Materials: 32 balls Lister 2-spun double-crêpe Tricel-with-nylon. Hooks as specified on page 44
Elastic for waist—68·5 cm (0·75 yd) of 2·5 cm (1 in.)

Tension: see page 44
Abbreviations: see page 13

The jacket back

Using No 4·50 hook, make 77ch.

1st row 1tr into 4th ch from hook, * 2ch, miss 2 ch, 1dc into next ch, 2ch, miss 2 ch, 1tr into each of next 6ch, rep from * to last 7ch, 2ch, miss 2ch, 1dc into next ch, 2ch, miss 2ch, 1tr into each of next 2ch, 3ch, turn.

2nd row Miss 1tr, 1tr into next tr, * (1ch, 1dc into sp) twice, 1ch, miss 1tr, 3tr in next tr, miss 2tr, 3tr into next tr, rep from * ending (1ch, 1dc into sp) twice, 1ch, 1tr into each of next 2tr, 3ch, turn.

3rd row Miss 1tr, 1tr into next tr, * 2ch, 1dc into sp between 2dc, 2ch, (3tr into centre tr of 3tr block) twice, rep from * ending 2ch, 1dc into sp between 2dc, 2ch, 1tr into each of next 2tr, 3ch, turn.

4th row Miss 1tr, 1tr into next tr, * (3tr into 2ch sp) twice, 2ch, 1dc between 3tr blocks, 2ch, rep from * ending (3tr into 2ch sp) twice, 1tr into each of next 2tr, 3ch, turn.

45

5th row Miss 1tr, 1tr into next tr, * (3tr into centre tr of 3tr block) twice, (1ch, 1dc into 2ch sp) twice, 1ch, rep from * ending (3tr into centre tr of 3tr block) twice, 1tr into each of next 2tr, 3ch, turn.

6th row Miss 1tr, 1tr into next tr, * (3tr into centre tr of 3tr block) twice, 2ch, 1dc into sp between 2dc, 2ch, rep from * ending (3tr into centre tr of 3tr block) twice, 1tr into each of next 2tr, 3ch, turn.

7th row Miss 1tr, 1tr into next tr, * 2ch, 1dc between 3tr blocks, 2ch, (3tr into 2ch sp) twice, rep from * ending 2ch, 1dc between 3tr blocks, 2ch, 1tr into each of next 2tr, 3ch, turn.

Rows 2 to 7 form the pattern. Continue in pattern until work measures 34·3 cm (13·5 in.) ending with a 6th row, and omitting 3ch at end of last row.

Shape armholes
With right side facing, next row: ss across 6tr, 3ch, miss 1tr, 1tr into next tr, * (3tr into 2ch sp) twice, 2ch, 1dc between 3tr blocks, 2ch, rep from * 4 times more, (3tr into 2ch sp) twice, 1tr into each of next 2tr, 3ch, turn.
Now continue in pattern until work measures 54·5 cm (21·5 in.) from beginning.
Shape shoulders
Ss across 6sts, pattern to last 6sts. Fasten off.

Jacket right front
Using No 4·50 hook, ch 46.
1st row   1tr into 4th ch from hook, 1tr into each of next 2ch, * 2ch, miss 2ch, 1dc into next ch, 2ch, miss 2ch, 1tr into each of next 6ch, rep from * to last 7ch, 2ch, miss 2ch, 1dc into next ch, 2ch, miss 2ch, 1tr into each of next 2ch, 3ch, turn.
2nd row Miss 1tr, 1tr into next tr, * (1ch, 1dc into sp) twice, 1ch, miss 1tr, 3tr into next tr, miss 2tr, 3tr into next tr, rep from * ending (1ch, 1dc into sp) twice, 1ch, 1tr into each of next 4tr, 3ch, turn.
The pattern for the right front is now set with 4tr at centre front edge. Continue in pattern until work measures 34·3 cm (13·5 in.) from beginning.

Shape armhole
Right side facing
Next row   Pattern to last 5sts, turn.
Continue in pattern until work measures 52 cm (20·5 in.) from beginning.

Shape neck

Right side facing.
Ss across 13sts (counting ch, dc, or tr each one as one st) pattern

46

to end.
Next row Pattern to last 5sts, turn.

Shape shoulder
Next row Pattern to last 6sts. Fasten off.

Jacket left front
Using No 4·50 hook, ch 46.
1st row 1tr into 4th ch from hook, * 2ch, miss 2ch, 1dc into next ch, 2ch, miss 2ch, 1tr into each of next 6ch, rep from * to last 9ch, 2ch, miss 2ch, 1dc into next ch, 2ch, miss 2ch, 1tr into each of next 4ch, 3ch, turn.
2nd row Miss 1tr, 1tr into each of next 3tr, * (1ch, 1dc into sp) twice, 1ch, miss 1tr, 3tr into next tr, miss 2tr, 3tr into next tr, rep from * ending (1ch, 1dc into sp) twice, 1ch, 1tr into each of next 2tr, 3ch, turn.
The pattern for left front is now set with 4tr at centre front edge.
Now work to correspond with right front, reversing all shapings.

The sleeves
The width of these will be graduated by changes in hook size from No 4·00, to 4·50 and 5·00.
Using No 4·00 hook, ch 55, and work in pattern as for back until 3 complete patterns have been worked.
Change to No 4·50 hook and continue in pattern until 6 patterns have been completed.
Change to No 5·00 hook and continue in pattern until work measures 35·5 cm (14 in.) from beginning.
Now work 3 more rows in pattern, increasing 1tr at each end of every row (keeping increased sts in tr), then work 3 more rows in pattern (still keeping 5tr at each end of rows). Fasten off.

TO MAKE UP
Read intructions for pressing the type of yarn used. Pin out and press each piece according to instructions.
  Join shoulder and side seams. Join sleeve seams to within 3·8 cm (1·5 in.) of top.
  Set in sleeves, placing centre of head of sleeve to shoulder seam and joining 3·8 cm (1·5 in.) left open at top of sleeve to beginning of armhole shaping on back and fronts.

Edging for lower edge
Rejoin yarn to lower edge of left front. Using No 4·50 hook, work edging of 5 dbl tr into one st, then work 1dc, continue thus, leaving sps of 1·9 cm (0·75 in.) between shell and dc along lower edge, turn.
Next row Work 1dc, 1ch into each st. Fasten off.
Work edging round neck and sleeve edges.
Press seams and edgings.

Sew on 4 buttons to correspond with sps in pattern which will form buttonholes.

The buttons
Using No 4·00 hook, ch 4, and join with ss to form a ring.
1st round   8tr into ring.
2nd and 3rd rounds   Work 1tr into each tr of previous round. Break off yarn, and thread through last round of tr, fill button with a length of same yarn, draw up, and fasten off securely.

The skirt (2 pieces)
Using No 5·00 hook, ch 88, and work in pattern as for back until work measures 20·3 cm (8 in.). The length may be adjusted at this point.
Change to No 4·50 hook, and continue in pattern until work measures 38 cm (15 in.) from beginning.
Change to No 4·00 hook and continue in pattern until work measures 58·5 cm (23 in.). Fasten off.

TO MAKE UP
Pin out and press each piece according to instructions.
   Join side seams. Join elastic to form a circle, and work herringbone stitch over elastic to encase it.
   Using No 4·50 hook, work edging as given for lower edge of jacket. Press seams and edging.

Man's sweater

Crocheted garments and crochet work are not now regarded as the exclusive province of woman. In the past many men, particularly Naval types, have passed away their time by hooking most exquisite examples of the handicraft. Today crochet is taught and worked as therapy in many institutions, including some of H. M. Prisons, where people of both sexes have excelled themselves in the work they have done.

Although the more elaborate crochet patterns are best suited to women's wear, it seems only fair to provide something in this section of the book for the man of the house. He may even decide to make it himself. The raglan sweater (see plate 14), with slight contrast relief round neck and waist, is a good basic pattern on which to work. Extra care must be taken in shaping the raglan edges, by decreasing one stitch within the edges, as neatness in joining up is essential to give a professional finish.

The knitted ribbing at waist, cuffs and neck, worked when the crochet is completed, provides better elasticity than crochet stitches, and the combination of both handicrafts in the garment shows how well the two can be united.

This design can easily be converted into a V-necked sweater, a cardigan, a sleeveless slipover or a jumper with inset sleeves. Incidentally, it looks equally attractive when worn by a woman.

MEASUREMENTS
Chest 101–107 cm (40–42 in.)
Length from shoulder 67·3 cm (26·5 in.)
Undersleeve seam 45·7 cm (18 in.)

YARN
Lister Lavenda double-crêpe wool was chosen as it is very
hardwearing, warm and above all, easy on the hook.

STITCH PATTERN
This is a simple 2-row pattern (see Fig. 14) consisting of one row
entirely of trebles followed by a 7-stitch combination of (4tr,
1sp, 1 bobble, 1sp), giving a vertical, self-colour striped effect.

HOOK TEST
With a No 4·00 hook and working over 4 patterns and 14 rows
1 pattern = 3·8 cm (1·5 in.)
6 rows = 6·3 cm (2·5 in.)

PLANNING THE SWEATER
The back
Begin with No 4·00 hook and 99-chain foundation. This will
provide 98 trebles, making 13 complete stitch-patterns with 2
trebles at each edge. When the seams are joined these 2 trebles
will unite with 2 trebles each side of the front, making a complete 4-treble block.

Underarm shaping involves decreasing 9 stitches each end
after the 35th row, followed by raglan shaping at each end of
every row to 32 stitches for back neck.

The front
This is worked as the back, including underarm decreases and
raglan, until 50 stitches remain.

Fig. 14. The 2-row pattern for the
man's sweater.

For the neck shaping 15 stitches will be left at centre, raglan shaping continuing through neck shaping to end of stitches.

The sleeves

For each sleeve begin with 50 chain, giving 6 patterns, with 4 stitches each end to form one pattern.

Shaping is worked by increasing 1 stitch each end every 3rd row to 71 stitches. Work plain to 40·7 cm (16 in.) from beginning and raglan shape as for the back until 5 stitches remain.

Fig. 15. The 4-piece man's sweater drawn to scale, with the test piece alongside.

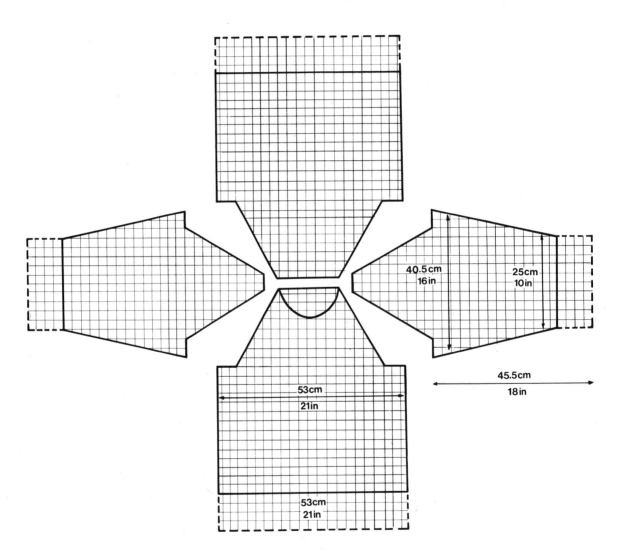

40.5 cm
16 in

25 cm
10 in

45.5 cm
18 in

53 cm
21 in

53 cm
21 in

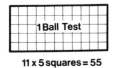

1 Ball Test

11 x 5 squares = 55

The welts

These are worked on to the edges of the crochet at the lower edge of the sweater, round the cuffs and round the neck.

For the lower edge, begin with No 11 knitting needles and 126 stitches. Twenty one rows should be worked, with a contrast wool stripe at two points. Sleeve bands are worked over 68 stitches for 21 rows, and the neck band has 9 rows with one contrast stripe.

TEST FOR YARN REQUIREMENT

With a No 4·00 hook 56 trebles were worked into a foundation chain of 57. The test measured 28 cm (11 in.) × 12·5 cm (5 in.).

Diagram on graph paper

Figure 15 shows the 4-piece sweater drawn to scale, with the test piece alongside.

Total number of squares on sweater	1,257
Total number of squares on test	55
Number of balls required for sweater (1,257 ÷ 55)	22·8 balls
To nearest ball	23·0 balls
Add 2 balls for welts	25·0 balls

An oddment, if available, will supply sufficient wool for the contrast, otherwise you will need 1 ball of contrast.

TO MAKE THE SWEATER

Measurements: as on page 49
Materials: 25 balls Lister Lavenda double-crêpe for main colour; 1 ball, or an oddment, of contrast colour; No 4·00 crochet hook; 1 pair knitting needles, size 11.
Tension: see page 49
Abbreviations: see page 13

Back

With No 4·00 hook and M colour, 99ch, turn.

1st row   (right side) Miss 2ch, 1tr into each ch to end, 2ch, turn.

2nd row   Miss 1tr, 1tr into next tr, * 1ch, miss 1tr, 1B into next tr. This is made by (yoh, hook into st to be worked and draw up a lp) 3 times, yoh and draw through all 7sts on hook, secure with 1ch), 1ch, miss 1tr, 1tr into each of next 4tr, rep from * to last 5tr, 1ch, miss 1tr, 1B into next tr, 1ch, miss 1tr, 1tr into each of next 2tr, 2ch, turn.

3rd row   Miss 1tr, 1tr into next tr, * 1tr into 1ch sp, 1tr into B, 1tr into 1ch sp, 1tr into each of next 4tr, rep from * ending 1tr into 1ch sp, 1tr into B, 1tr into 1ch sp, 1tr into each of next 2tr, 2ch, turn.

Rep last 2 rows until work measures 35·5 cm (14 in.) from beginning.

Shape raglan

With right side facing and keeping in pattern

Next row   Ss across 9sts, patt to last 9sts, 2ch, turn ** Continue in pattern, decreasing one st at each end of every row until 32sts remain, (1ch sp or 1 bobble are always counted as 1st). Fasten off.

Front
Work as back as far as **
Continue in pattern, decreasing 1st at each end of every row until 50sts remain.

Shape neck
With right side facing:
Next row   Miss 2tr, 1tr into each of next 15sts, turn.
Continue in pattern, shaping raglan as before, at same time decreasing 1st at neck edge on every row until all sts are worked off.
Return to remaining st, with right side facing miss 16sts, rejoin wool and work to correspond with other side.

Sleeves
With No 4·00 hook and M colour, 50ch, turn.
1st row   (right side) Miss 2ch, 1tr into each ch to end, 2ch, turn.
2nd and 3rd rows   As for back.
Now continue in pattern, increasing one st at each end of next and every following 3rd row until 71sts have been worked.
Continue in pattern until work measures 40·5 cm (16 in.) from beginning.

Shape raglan
As for back until 5sts remain. Fasten off.

Knitted ribs for lower edge of back and front
With right side facing, using No 11 needles and M colour, pick up and knit 126sts along lower edge. Work 7 rows in k1, p1 rib. Break off M colour. Join C shade.
Next row   Knit.
Next row   Work in rib. Break off C, join in M.
Next row   Knit.
Next 3 rows   Work in k1, p1 rib. Break off M, join in C.
Next row   Knit.
Next row   Work in rib. Break off, C, join in M.
Next row   Knit.
Next 5 rows   Work in rib. Cast off in rib.

Sleeve ribs
With right side facing, with No 11 needles and M colour, pick up and knit 68sts, and work 21 rows in rib as given for lower edge bands. Cast off in rib.

Plate 10 (*Left*) The panelled maxi-dress.

Plate 11 (*Above*) The six-hour waistcoat.

Plate 12 (*Below left*) Mother's and daughter's dresses.

Plate 13 (*Below right*) The lacey cardigan—skirt suit, for all-round-the-year wear.

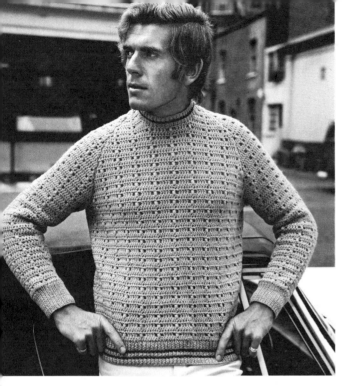

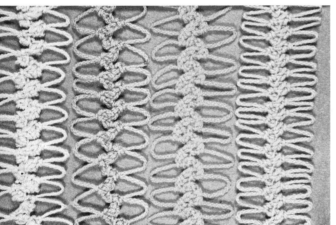

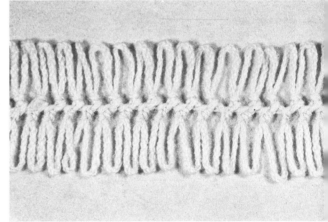

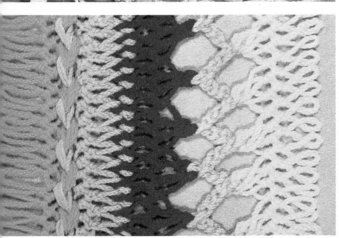

Plate 14 (*Top left*) Man's raglan sweater—simple 2-row pattern and knitted welts.

Plate 15 (*Top right*) Four Irish-type motifs joined together.

Plate 16 (*Centre left*) Various strips of hairpin crochet.

Plate 17 (*Above*) The double-crochet hairpin strip.

Plate 18 (*Left*) Methods of joining hairpin strips.

Neckband
Join raglan seams very neatly, leaving left back seam open.
With right side facing and beginning at top of left sleeve, rejoin
M colour, and with No 11 needles, pick up and knit 9sts at top of
sleeve; pick up and knit 64sts round front neck; pick up and knit
6sts across top of right sleeve; and finally pick up and knit 36sts
across back of neck (112sts).
Work 3 rows in k1, p1 rib. Break off M colour, join in C.
Next row   Knit.
Next row   Work in rib. Break off C, join in M.
Next row   Knit.
Work 3 rows in k1, p1 rib. Cast off in rib.

TO MAKE UP
Pin out and press each piece on wrong wide to correct measurement under a damp cloth, avoiding ribbed welts. (Or follow instructions for type of yarn used.)
Join remaining raglan seam. Join side and sleeve seams. Press
all seams.

Edward the Ted

Who would not adore this lovable, washable, durable, made-
in-an-evening, double-crochet bear (see Fig. 16). Economical
in yarn consumption, it would make any little girl or boy happy
as a day or bedtime playmate.

MEASUREMENTS
Height 41 cm (16 in.)
Head; all round over nose 33 cm (13 in.)
Forehead to neck 11·5 cm (4·5 in.)
Body height 15·25 cm (6 in.)
All round body, after stuffing 26·5 cm (10·5 in.)
Length of arms 12·5 cm (5 in.)
All round arms 9 cm (3·5 in.)
Length of legs 12·76 cm (5in.)
All round legs 10 cm (4 in.)

YARN
Lister Bri-nylon double-knitting (Harvest Gold). Oddment or 1
ball of dark brown or black for pads and features.

HOOK TEST
With No 3·50 hook and working over 20 double-crochet
stitches 5dc = 2·5 cm (1 in.)

PLANNING THE BEAR
The head and ears are worked with two strands throughout.
The head is worked in one piece, beginning at front neck and

Fig. 16. Edward the Ted, Lucky the lamb and Popette the poodle.

continuing over nose and down the back. The ears are worked separately and attached to the top of the head.

The body which is slightly shaped at lower end and neck, is made in two pieces and joined at the sides. The two legs and two arms have additional contrasting pads.

YARN REQUIREMENT

The head and ears	1·75 balls
Body	1·5 balls
Legs and arms	1·5 balls
Total	4·75 balls
To nearest ball	5·0 balls

The body is worked with a No 3·50 hook, as are the arms and legs. For the head the double yarn is worked with a No 4·00 hook. Double-crochet stitches are used throughout.

TO MAKE THE BEAR
Materials: 5 balls Bri-nylon yarn; 1 ball (or oddment) of dark

54

brown or black; 1 No 4·00 hook; 1 No 3·50 hook; 46 cm (18 in.) ribbon for necktie bow; Foam chippings or other suitable stuffing.

The head
With double yarn and No 4·00 hook, begin with 17ch.
1st row   1dc in 2nd ch from hook, 1dc in each ch to end, 1ch, turn.
2nd row   2dc in first dc, 1dc in each of next 5dc, 2dc in next dc, 1dc in each of next 2dc, 2dc in next dc, 1dc in each of next 5dc, 2dc in last dc, 1ch, turn.
3rd row   2dc in 1st dc, 1dc in each of next 7dc, 2dc in next dc, 1dc in each of next 2dc, 2dc in next dc, 1dc in each of next 7dc, 2dc in last dc, 1ch, turn.
4th to 7th rows, inclusive: All in dc straight.
8th row   1dc in each of next 9dc, miss 1dc, 1dc in each of next 4dc, miss 1dc, 1dc in each dc to end, 1ch, turn.
9th row   1dc in each of next 8dc, miss 1dc, 1dc in each of next 4dc, miss 1dc, 1dc in each dc to end, 1ch, turn.
Work next 26 rows straight in dc.
Next row   1dc in 1st dc, miss 1dc, 1dc in each of next 6dc, miss 1dc, 1dc in each of next 2dc, miss 1dc, 1dc in each of next 6dc, miss 1dc, 1dc in last dc.
Next row   All dc. Fasten off.
Fold in half, join side seams, and fill with stuffing.

The ears (2)
Begin with 10ch.
1st row   1dc in 2nd ch from hook, 1dc in every ch to end, 1ch, turn.
Work next 15 rows straight all in dc. Fasten off.
Fold in half and join seam. Do not break off yarn but pull up slightly, and sew ears to head.

The body
Begin with 17ch.
1st row   1dc in 2nd ch from hook, 1dc in each ch to end, 1ch, turn.
2nd row   2dc in 1st dc, 1dc in each dc to last st, 2dc in last st, 1ch, turn.
Next row   All dc, 1ch, turn.
Rep last 2 rows until there are 26sts. Work 19 rows dc.
Next row   1dc in 1st dc, miss 1dc, 1dc in each dc to last 2dc, miss 1dc, 1dc in last dc, 1ch, turn.
Next row   All dc, 1ch, turn.
Rep last 2 rows until 18sts remain. Fasten off.
Work another piece exactly the same. Sew together, leave an opening, and fill with stuffing.

The legs (2)
Begin with 25ch.
1st row   1dc in 2nd ch from hook, 1dc in each ch to end, 1ch,
turn.
Work 4 rows in dc.
Next row   1dc in each of next 12dc, miss next 2dc, 1dc in each
dc to end, 1ch, turn.
Next row   1dc in each of next 10dc, miss next 2dc, 1dc in each
dc to end, 1ch, turn.
Work 18 rows in dc. Fasten off. Join long sides together, and
stuff.

The pads (2)
Using dark colour, begin with 8ch.
1st row   1dc in 2nd ch from hook, 1dc in each ch to end, 1ch,
turn.
2nd row   2dc in 1st dc, 1dc in each of next 5dc, 2dc in last dc,
1ch, turn.
3rd row   2dc in 1st dc, 1dc in each of next 7dc, 2dc in last dc,
1ch, turn.
4th row   1dc in 1st dc, miss 1dc, 1dc in each of next 7dc, miss
1dc, 1dc in last dc, 1ch, turn.
5th row   1dc in 1st dc, miss 1dc, 1dc in each of next 5dc, miss
1dc, 1dc in last dc. Fasten off.
Sew the pads to lower edge of legs, and sew legs to body towards
the front.

The arms
Begin with 19ch.
1st row   1dc in 2nd ch from hook, 1dc in each ch to end, 1ch,
turn.
Work 20 rows in dc.
Next row * 1dc in each of next 9dc, 1ch, turn.
Next row   Miss 1st dc, 1dc in each of next 6dc, miss next dc,
1dc in last dc, turn.
Next row   All dc.
Rep last 2 rows until only 3sts remain. Fasten off.
Join in dark colour and rep from *.
Join long sides together, leave top open, and stuff. Attach
towards front of body.

TO COMPLETE
Join head to body, tie neat ribbon bow round neck.
   Using dark yarn, sew features—nose, mouth eyes etc., as
shown in Fig. 16.

Irish crochet

Irish crochet ranks high among the most beautiful in the world. The history of the handicraft is obscure, but the making of Irish lace can be traced as far back as 1672. In that year it was recorded that a special class for crochet was included in a needlework exhibition in Dublin.

It is also known that by 1845, and for many subsequent years, crochet became a flourishing national industry in Ireland. This was almost certainly encouraged by the French nuns who arrived there, and probably taught the skills to children in the convents of the land.

The enthusiastic designer will, no doubt, be able to discover more and, with experience, will be able to produce variations on the basic, very beautiful patterns.

In this section of the book fashion has, so far, dominated the scene, but we must not forget that the domestic front, too, can be greatly enhanced by crocheted works of art. It was, after all, in this field that crochet was most prominent in ages past. With today's lovely yarns there is literally no limit to the things that a

Fig. 17. Teacloth with Irish-crochet corners and edging.

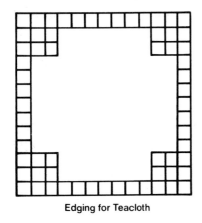

Edging for Teacloth

Fig. 18. Positioning the rose motifs for the teacloth.

pair of energetic hands can accomplish.

The teacloth pictured in Fig. 17 bears this out. This particular kind of covering has, to some extent, vanished from many tables in favour of mats. When a cloth worked in crochet does appear, however, it seldom fails to invoke the admiration and 'how I wish I could do it' from visiting friends.

The edging of the cloth shown is designed in a modern version of a traditional Irish rose motif, with the accent on each corner where several motifs are joined in square formation, as illustrated in Fig. 18.

The body of the cloth can be made of any suitable linen or other material, and looks particularly attractive if motifs and mounting are designed to complement the décor of the room.

Other well-known Irish motifs include the ring, the wheel, the shamrock, single or triple leaf and many variations (see plate 15). They can be used individually, or set in a background of their own traditional plain lace, examples of which appear on pages 60 and 61. For the motif used in the cloth, double-picot background lace is used in conjuntion with the rose.

MOTIFS FOR THE TEACLOTH
It will be seen from Fig. 18 that 1 square represents 1 rose motif. There will be a single row of motifs surrounding the cloth, with 4 extra motifs inset at each corner, making a total of 64 motifs.

The first motif
For an illustration of this, see Fig. 19. Using a No 1·00 hook and Coats Mercer crochet cotton No 40 (weight: 20 gm per ball), begin with 15ch and join with 1ss to form a ring.

1st round Into ring work 24dc, 1ss into first dc.

2nd round 1dc into same place as last ss, * 5ch, miss 2dc, 1dc into next dc, rep from * ending with 5ch, 1ss into first dc (8 loops made).

3rd round Into each loop work 1dc, 1hlf tr, 5tr, 1hlf tr, 1dc, (8 petals), 1ss into first dc.

4th round * 5ch, 1dc into next dc of round before last, inserting hook from back, rep from * ending with 5ch.

5th round Into each lp work 1dc 1hlf tr 7tr 1hlf tr 1dc, 1ss into first dc.

6th round As 4th having 7ch lps instead of 5ch.

7th round Into each lp work 1dc 1hlf tr 9tr 1hlf tr 1dc, 1ss into first dc.

8th round 1dc into same place as last ss, * 5ch into centre st of petal work 1tr 5ch 1tr, 5ch, 1dc between petals, 3ch, 1ss into 3rd ch from hook, 5ch, 1ss into 3rd ch from hook, 1ch (a picot lp made), 1dc into centre st of next petal, 1 picot lp, 1dc between next 2 petals, rep from * omitting 1dc at end of last rep, 1ss into first dc.

9th round 1ss into each of next 4ch, 1dc in to lp, * into next lp work 1dc 1hlf tr 9tr 1hlf tr 1dc, 1dc into next 5ch lp, (1 picot lp,

58

Fig. 19. The rose motif.

1dc between picots of next lp) twice, 1 picot lp, 1dc into next 5ch lp, rep from * omitting 1dc at end of last rep, 1ss into first dc.

10th round   1ss into each of next 2 sts, 1dc into next st, * 5ch, into centre tr of same petal work 1tr 5ch and 1tr, 5ch, miss 3sts, 1dc into next st, (1 picot lp, 1dc between picots of next lp) 3 times, 1 picot lp, 1dc into first tr of next corner group, rep from * omitting 1dc at end of last rep, 1ss into first dc.

11th round   1ss into each of next 4ch, 1dc into lp, * into next lp work 1dc 1hlf tr 9tr 1hlf tr and 1dc, 1dc into next 5ch lp, (1 picot lp, 1dc between picots of next lp) 4 times, 1 picot lp, 1dc into next 5ch lp, rep from * omitting 1dc at end of last rep, 1ss into first dc.

12th round   As 10th round having 6 picot lps on each side instead of 4.

13th round   As 11th round having 7 picot lps on each side instead of 5. Fasten off.

Second motif
Work same as first motif for 12 rounds.

13th round   1ss into each of next 4ch, 1dc into lp, into next lp work 1dc 1hlf tr 8tr, remove hook, insert hook into corresponding tr of corner group of first motif and draw dropped lp through, 1tr 1hlf tr and 1dc into same lp on second motif, 1dc into next 5ch lp, * 3ch, 1ss into 3rd ch from hook, 1ch, 1dc betwen picots of next lp on first motif, 3ch, 1ss into 3rd ch from

hook, 1ch, 1dc into centre of next lp on second motif, rep from
* 6 times more, 1dc 1hlf tr and 1tr into next lp, remove hook, insert hook into corresponding tr of next corner group of first
motif and draw dropped lp through, 8tr, 1hlf tr and 1dc into
same lp on second motif and complete as for first motif.
Make and join subsequent motifs in the same way.

MOTIF TEST FOR YARN REQUIREMENT
4 test motifs were made according to instructions.

Weight of 4 motifs	9·6 gm
Weight of 1 motif	2·4 gm
Weight of 64 motifs	153·6 gm
Number of 20-gm balls required	7·6 balls
To nearest ball	8·0 balls

Measurement of each motif	7·75 cm (3·125 in.)
Size of cloth	107·0 cm (42·25 in.)

TO MAKE THE CLOTH
Make the motifs and join together as instructions. Follow Fig.
18 indicating the placing of the motifs, joining adjacent sides as
the second motif is joined to the first. Damp and pin out to
measurements.

Place edging on linen, or other material, trace outline and
mount as desired. Dampen and press.

IDEAS USING THE ROSE MOTIF
The rose-centre motif, probably the most popular of its type,
lends itself to the design of many beautiful things for the home
such as bedspreads, chair backs, table runners etc. It also works
well in thicker yarns; and can be adapted for fashion wear,
either for whole garments or as insertions in other fabrics.

OTHER BACKGROUND LACES

Chain lace
For an illustration of this, see Fig. 20.
Make a ch slightly longer than desired length of lace
1st row   1dc into 10th ch from hook, * 6ch, miss 3ch,
1dc into next ch, rep from * across chain, 9ch, turn.
2nd row   * 1dc into next lp, 6ch, rep from * across, ending with
6ch, 1dc into last lp, 9ch, turn.
Further rows   Rep 2nd row for length desired. Fasten off.

Loop lace
For an illustration of this, see Fig. 21.
Make a ch slightly longer than the desired length of lace
1st row   1dc into 15th ch from hook, 4ch, 1dc into same place,

60

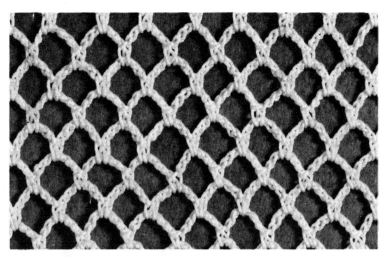

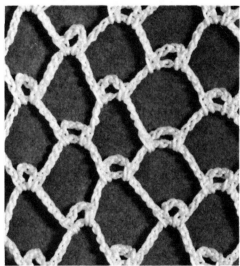

Fig. 20. Chain lace.

Fig. 21. Loop lace.

* 10ch, miss 6ch, 1dc 4ch 1dc into next ch, rep from * across, turn.

2nd row Ss to centre of 4ch lp, 13ch, * into next 10ch lp work 1dc 4ch and 1dc, 10ch, rep from * across, ending with 1dc 4ch 1dc into last lp, turn.

Further rows rep 2nd row as required.

Irish lace blouse

This blouse, for which working instructions appear on page 101, is an outstanding, exquisite example of the use of Irish lace in fashion wear, and it is well worth every minute of the time taken to produce it.

Trolley cloth

On page 117 Fig. 42 shows a distinctive trolley cloth with applied motifs in Irish lace.

A host of other articles will immediately spring to the mind of

Fig. 22. The hexagonal motif in Irish style.

the designer wishing to add distinction to the home.

HEXAGONAL MOTIF IN IRISH STYLE

This motif (see Fig. 22) could be substituted for the one used for the dress (page 23). Its picots and flat petalled edges, with four-chain loop fillings make it both attractive and easy to work.

First motif

Begin with 5ch.

1st row Into 5th ch from hook work (1tr, 2ch) 7 times, 1ss into 3rd of 5ch.

2nd row 1ss into first sp, 1dc into same sp, * (5ch, 1ss into 4th ch from hook—picot made—) twice, 1ch, 1dc into next sp, rep from * omitting 1dc at end of the last rep, 1ss into first dc.

3rd row Ss to ch between next 2 picots on next lp, 1dc into same lp, * 7ch, 1dc between picots of next lp, rep from * omitting 1dc at end of last rep, 1ss into first dc.

4th row Into each lp work (1dc 1hlf tr 9tr, 1hlf tr, 1dc), 1ss into first dc (8 petals). Fasten off.

Second motif

Work as first motif for 3 rows.

4th row Into first lp work 1dc, 1hlf tr, 4tr, 1ss into centre tr of a petal of first motif, 5tr, 1hlf tr, and 1dc into same lp on second motif, into next lp work 1dc 1hlf tr, 4tr, 1ss into centre tr of next petal on first motif, 5tr, 1hlf tr, and 1dc into same lp on second motif, finish as for first motif.

Filling
When four or more motifs are worked, the spaces between may be filled as follows:
Begin with 6ch, join with 1ss to form a ring.
1st row   1dc into ring, 4ch, 1ss into any join between motifs, 4ch, (1dc into ring, 4ch, 1ss into next joining between motifs, 4ch), 3 times, 1ss into first dc. Fasten off.

Filet crochet

Filet, the French word for net, is probably the oldest form of the crochet craft, and it is certainly a good one with which the not-too-experienced crocheter can begin to design.

Household articles of all kinds, and ecclesiastical laces, have always appeared in filet lace, but it is only in very recent years that it has crept into the modern home and personal fashion scene, due no doubt to the wonderful miscellany of yarns now available.

Filet is often worked from a chart, thus saving the time of both printer and crocheter by considerably reducing the written instructions. Treble and chain stitches form the greater part of the work, with lacets and bars added to relieve the block-and-space design. A single block of 4 trebles becomes a double block by the addition of 3 more trebles, the central (4th) treble standing for both blocks, and so on.

In some charts the blocks are denoted by shaded squares, in others a cross indicates their position, the spaces being left blank.

The filet curtains, pictured in Fig. 23 make a good stepping-off mark in this type of design. The actual design and colour of material used can be varied according to the ideas of the worker, who will no doubt have in mind the décor of the room they are destined to adorn.

It is perhaps not surprising that many women today, and even some handicraft-minded men, are returning to the production of their own crocheted curtains. In addition to the personal pride involved in working them for home use, it has been discovered that machine-made curtain nets of synthetic materials do lose their freshness after constant laundering. Crocheted curtains, however, made from any modern plain white or colourfast materials can be washed repeatedly, boiled, and starched again and again. They will reappear at the windows sparkling fresh and crease and dust resistant—a boon to any busy housewife.

When calculating yarn requirement, the best way is to work a whole ball from beginning to end, and then assess the ap-

Fig. 23. Filet-crochet curtains.

proximate total consumption by comparative measurement, bearing in mind variations in pattern as work progresses.

MATERIALS
The cotton chosen was Coats Mercer Crochet No 40; hook size 1·00.

TENSION TEST
A test piece was worked over 30 spaces to 30 rows produced a tension of 6 spaces and 6 rows = 2·5 cm (1 in.)

Another small test, taken over a series of blocks and spaces, showed that 1 block consumed approximately the same amount of cotton as 2 spaces.

WORKING DETAILS
The flower design with castellated border is a simple yet very attractive one with which to begin. It is composed simply of blocks and plenty of spaces, and can be followed easily from the chart (Fig. 24).

Size of window to be curtained 101·5 cm (40 in.) wide × 96·5 cm

64

(38 in.) deep.

Each curtain will cover an area 50·7 cm (20 in.) wide × 94·5 cm (37·33 in.) deep, giving 1·7 cm (0·66 in.) clearance at the base. Actual size of each curtain 67·0 cm (26 in.) wide × 95·0 cm (37·5 in.) deep.

At 6 sps per 2·5 cm (1 in.), the number of blocks and spaces required to begin the lower edge of one curtain will be 168.

At 6 rows per 2·5 cm (1 in.), the number of rows required will be 6 × 37·33 = 224 rows.

For the top casing turn-down 4 rows must be added, making the total number of rows required 228.

TO MAKE THE CURTAINS

Begin with 1 new ball of cotton and work until the end, with 482ch.

1st row   1tr into 8th ch from hook, * 2ch, miss 2ch, 1tr in next ch (sp made), 1tr in each of next 9ch (3 blks made), rep from * 38 times more, (2ch, miss 2ch, 1tr into next ch) twice, 5ch, turn.

2nd row   Miss first tr, 1tr into next tr (sp made at beginning of row), 2ch, 1tr into next tr (sp made over sp), 1tr into each of next 3tr (blk made over blk), 2ch, miss 2tr, 1tr into next tr (sp made over blk), * 1 blk, 1sp, rep from * 76 times, 2ch, miss 2ch, 1tr into next ch (sp made at end of row) 3ch, turn.

3rd row   Miss first tr, 2tr into next sp, 1tr into next tr (blk made at beginning of row), 2tr into next sp, 1tr into next tr (blk made over sp), * 1 blk, 1sp, rep from * 76 times more, 2 blks, 2tr into next sp, 1tr into 3rd of 5ch (blk made at end of row), 3ch, turn. From this point on, follow diagram from 4th to 43rd row, rep 24th to 43 rows 7 times more, then 24th row to end. Fasten off. Work another identical curtain.

TO MAKE UP

Damp and pin out to correct measurements. Turn back the last 4 rows and slip stitch neatly in to place to form the top casing.

YARN REQUIREMENT

The first ball, largely on account of the number of blocks in the rows, worked to the end of the 11th row; the second ball to the 25th row.

The 3rd ball will work a further 32 rows; the 4th another 32 rows, and so on to the top of the curtain, using a total of 8·25 balls as follows:

1st ball to row 12; 2nd ball to row 25; 3rd ball to row 57; 4th ball to row 89; 5th ball to row 121; 6th ball to row 153; 7th ball to row 185; 8th ball to row 217; 9th ball to row 226.

From the last ball 9 rows only are worked, i.e. approx one quarter of the ball.

The second curtain will take the same amount of cotton, so 17 balls will be sufficient to complete both curtains.

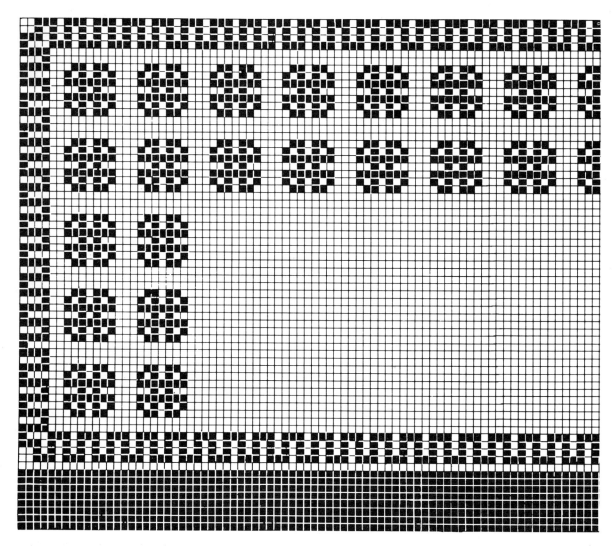

Fig. 24. Pattern-chart for the filet-crochet curtains.

Note: The curtains can be made longer or shorter by the addition or subtraction of middle sections. Also the spaces provide ample room for manoeuvre, and other designs can easily be substituted.

MORE IDEAS
Why not personalize household items, gifts, children's garments and so on with filet lace?

Either the dog (see Fig. 25) or duck (see Fig. 26) is ideal for a child's pullover or jacket, and the simple lettering (see Fig. 27) can easily be worked out for any of the letters of the alphabet and adapted in many different ways to suit individual taste.

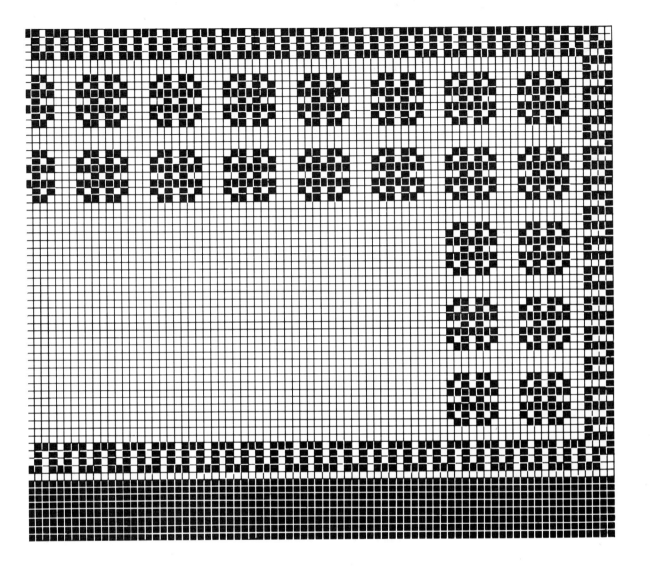

Fig. 25. Pattern for the filet-lace dog.   **Fig. 26.** Pattern for the filet-lace duck.   **Fig. 27.** Pattern for simple lettering in filet lace.

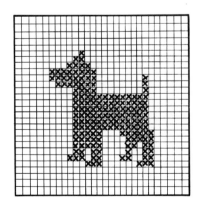

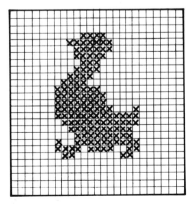

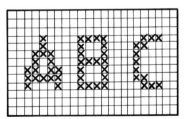

Weaving

Weaving on crochet (see Fig. 28) gives a completely new look to the handicraft, and it is so simple to do that even a beginner can achieve quite spectacular results.

The weaving can be worked over almost any background from plain trebles to more intricate patterns, and there is no end to the variety of designs to which this comparatively new aspect of crochet work can be adapted. A dainty or substantial stole, a jacket, suit, blanket or car rug, and many more items can be made quickly and easily. Fringed articles in particular lend themselves to this art form, as the ends can be left and knotted when weaving has been completed. The child's skirt, which can be enlarged to any size, is an elementary example with which to begin.

MEASUREMENTS
Waist 38 cm (15 in.)
Length 24 cm (9·5 in.) including waistband and lower edging
All round lower edge 84 cm (33 in.)

Note: The skirt should fit a child aged between 3 and 6 years.

YARN
Lee Target Titania double crêpe for the main colour and three contrasting colours.

HOOK TEST
Using a No 4·00 hook for the background of 1 treble, 1 chain, 3tr 2sp = 2·5 cm (1 in.) in width.

PLANNING THE SKIRT
The skirt will consist of one oblong 72-space piece of background fabric, (1tr, 1ch, 1tr) mesh. The waistband will be made in dc stitches, and for easy access the skirt will have a back seam with 4 buttons or a zip fastener.

The lower edging will be (1dc, 3ch, 1dc) evenly spaced.

3 strands of each of 3 colours will be woven vertically from the lower edge to the top of skirt mesh, shown in Fig. 28. If desired, instead of fastening off the strands at lower edge, these

Fig. 28. Weaving on crochet.

can be knotted, but extra yarn must be allowed for this before cutting.

YARN REQUIREMENT
Main colour:
1 ball worked 10 rows of background of 72 spaces.
For the 26 rows required for length, plus waistband and edgings at lower edge and back, 3 balls will be needed.
Contrast colours:
Oddments can be used, but if these are not available, 1 ball of each shade will be required.

TO MAKE THE SKIRT
Measurements: see page 68
Materials: 3 balls of Lee Target Titania double crêpe for the main colour (M); 1 ball each of the three contrast colours for weaving (C1, C2, C3); Crochet hooks 4·00 and 3·50; 4 buttons or a 10 cm (4 in.) zip fastener; 1 tapestry needle.

Note: When working into a treble stitch, always take into the hook the 3 strands at the top of treble of previous row, thus ensuring complete symmetry of each space. Do not weave too tightly or the garment will be misshapen.

Using M yarn, make 146ch.
1st row   1tr into 4th ch from hook (this allows for first tr, 1sp), (miss 1ch, 1tr) to end of ch (72sps). 4ch, turn.
2nd row   Miss 1sp, 1tr into next tr, (1ch, miss 1sp, 1tr into next tr) rep to end, 4ch, turn.
Rep 2nd row 24 times (26 rows total), omitting last 4 turning ch. Do not break off yarn.

Waistband
1st row   Work 1dc into each tr and 1dc into each sp to end of row.
2nd to 6th rows   Rep 1st row, break off yarn.

To weave
Cut strands as follows:
72 strands each of C1, C2 and C3, 30 cm (12 in.) long. Pin out and press garment according to instructions for yarn, making sure all spaces are symmetrical.

Beginning at lower edge, using a tapestry needle and 3 strands of C1, weave vertically over and under the 1ch bars. Using C2, weave another row similarly adjacent to C1, alternating the weaving. Using C3, work another row adjacent to C2. Repeat until all spaces have been woven into. Press very lightly on wrong side, after fastening off all ends neatly and securely.

Join back seam to within 10 cm (4 in.) of top. Work 2 rows dc evenly along left (button) side of opening. Work 1 row dc evenly along right side of opening, and on the 2nd row work 4 3ch button-holes evenly.

With No 3·50 hook, round lower edge of skirt work (1dc, 3ch, 1dc) into 1st evenly, for scalloped edging. Fasten off.

Hairpin crochet

Hairpin crochet is a special type of work which almost slipped into oblivion with the whole handicraft. It consists of strips of gimp made with a crochet hook on a U-shaped tool, known as a 'hairpin'. The bands are worked by winding the yarn around the prongs of the pin, fixing it in the centre with crochet stitches. The width of gimp depends upon the size of hairpin used (see plate 16). These sizes are given on page 131.

Hairpin work is reasonably economical in yarn consumption, is quite easy to make, and grows quickly after a little practice. The strips may be made with any yarn, from the finest cottons to thicker qualities, including any of the metallic threads so popular today in fashionwear.

Used separately, the gimp makes attractive belts, bracelets and even garters. Joined together, almost any size and shape can emerge, from gossamer stoles to the snuggest of blankets. Gimp in its plainest form is described here, with suggestions for more elaborate patterns and joinings. No doubt the keen designer will quickly discover some others of the infinite variety of patterns in this recently revived and versatile handicraft.

TO MAKE THE GIMP
Note:

1. Always work with a strong, rigid hairpin, otherwise as work progresses towards the top of the pin the loops will tend to pull the prongs inward, thus making shorter loops than those at the lower end.

2. When the gimp is being made, all loops should rest firmly, but not too tightly, against the prongs.

3. Unless a particular pattern states otherwise, the central 'spine' of the gimp should be made equidistant from both prongs.

4. To stop loops curling round on removal from the pin, run a length of contrast coloured yarn through the loops just before slipping them off.

Dc strip
This is shown in plate 17.

Make a slip-loop near end of yarn and, holding hook in right hand, slip loop on to hook. Hold hairpin in left hand between thumb and forefinger, with open end upwards and squared base in the hand.

With loop on hook, wind yarn round right prong of pin, yoh, and draw through loop on hook, keeping loop at centre of hair-

Fig. 29. Drawing through yarn from the right prong of the hairpin.

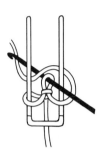

Fig. 30. The hairpin has been turned and the yarn wrapped round the left prong.

Fig. 31. The yarn has been pulled through and the loop centred.

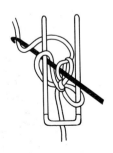

Fig. 32. Drawing the yarn through the two loops.

pin (see Fig. 29).

 * Raise hook to vertical position and turn pin round to the left, yoh, and draw through loop on hook. (See Figs 30 and 31.)

 Insert hook into loop on left prong, yoh, (Fig. 32) and draw loop through (2 loops on hook), yoh, and draw through these 2 loops (1dc made).

 Repeat from * until the hairpin is almost filled with loops, remove all loops, replacing the last 3 or 4 carefully each side to their respective prongs, and continue working for length required.

Alternative centres for strips

Instead of simple working 1dc into left prong loop:

 1. Work 2dc each time
 2. Work (1tr, 2ch, 1tr).
 3. Work (1dc, 3ch, 1dc)
 4. Work (1dc, 1tr, 1dc).

JOINING THE STRIPS
See plate 18.

Weaving, or plaiting

Place 2 strips side by side on a flat surface. Take into the hook the first 3 loops (untwisted) from one side, then take the corresponding 3 loops from the other side into the hook, pull second 3 loops through the first 3; now take the next 3 loops from first side and draw these through those already on hook. Continue in this manner until all loops are united. Fasten off securely using a spare piece of yarn. See child's cape, page 72 and bolero, page 74.

Chain

Place 2 strips side by side on flat surface, insert hook into first loop of one piece and draw through first loop of second piece; draw next loop of first piece through this loop, and continue until all loops are fixed, fasten off as before.

Twisted double-crochet chain

A contrasting coloured yarn used for this makes an attractive finish. Join yarn with a loop, take 3 loops twisted once from one strip, work 1dc 3ch, pick up corresponding 3 loops similarly twisted from the other strip, 1dc 3ch, and repeat to end of loops. Fasten off as before.

Child's cape or skirt

This attractive, colourful cape, which readily adapts to a skirt, will keep little backs or 'tums' very snug and warm.

It will fit any child between the ages of 3 and 6 years. The length and width can be altered to any size by adding more strips and further loops to each strip.

MEASUREMENTS
Length, including fringe 30·5 cm (12 in.)
Chest 51–63·5 cm (20–25 in.)
Hips 71–76·5 cm (28–30 in.)

CHOICE OF YARN
Lister Lavenda double-crêpe wool in 2 colours.

HOOK TEST
With a No 4·00 hook and a 60 (2·5 in.) hairpin, a test of 2 strips, each 20 loops each prong, woven together 3 × 3.
Tension 6 loops = 2·5 cm (1 in.)
2 woven strips = 7·75 cm (3 in.) wide
1 woven strip = 3·87 cm (1·5 in.) wide

Note: If the garment is to be enlarged, it will be necessary to add the following:
For every extra 3·87 cm (1·5 in.) length, add 1 strip.
For every extra 2·5 cm (1 in.) width, add 6 loops each prong.

PLANNING THE GARMENT
The garment will consist of 10 strips of varying lengths, woven 3 × 3 alternately to give a two-colour plaited effect, in horizontal formation. (See Fig. 33.)

According to the tension test, the following strips will be required, beginning at the top of the garment, and ending at lower edge:

2 strips 126 loops each prong, in First Colour
1 strip 126 loops each prong, in Second Colour
3 strips 168 loops each prong, in First Colour
3 strips 168 loops each prong, in Second Colour
1 strip 112 loops each prong, in 1 strand each colour for lowest fringed strip

Fig. 33. The two-colour pattern for the child's cape or skirt.

YARN REQUIREMENT

The 1-ball test worked 230 loops on each prong.

Total number of loops each prong to be worked:

First Colour (868) $868 \div 230 = 3 \cdot 7$ balls

Second Colour (742) $742 \div 230 = 3 \cdot 2$ balls

The small amount of each ball remaining will be sufficient to work front borders, draw-cord and tassels.

Total amount required: First Colour 4 balls

Second Colour 4 balls

TO MAKE THE GARMENT

Materials: 4 balls Lister Lavenda double crêpe: First Colour; 4 balls Lister Lavenda double crêpe: Second Colour; 1 crochet hook No 4·00 for hairpin; 1 crochet hook No 3·50 for borders; 1 hairpin size 60 (2·5 in.); 5 buttons.

Work all the strips as planned, making the dc centre of the 112-loop, 2-colour fringe strip 1·25 cm (0·5 in.) from left prong, thus giving sufficient length on loops the other side for the fringe.

To join the strips

Beginning with the two top strips of 126 loops, one of each colour, place the first strip alongside the second on a flat surface.

Keeping all loops straight (without twisting), take the first 3 loops from the first strip into the hook, then take the corresponding 3 of second strip into the hook, draw first 3 loops through second 3. Then take next 3 loops of first strip through those already on hook. Continue in this manner until all loops are woven. Fasten off securely using a spare piece of wool.

Similarly, take a third strip of first colour, 126 loops, and join to second strip.

Now take the first 168-strip of second colour, and weave 4 loops of this strip each time with 3 loops of previous strip. Join remaining 168-loop strips, taking 4 loops with 4, alternating the colours.

To join the fringe strip, weave the 2 shorter loops of this 112-loop, 2-colour strip with 3 loops of last 168-loop strip, to end. Cut through loops at lower edge for fringe.

Using No 3·50 hook, work 4 rows dc evenly along left front of garment. Work the same number of dc along right front for 2 rows; for buttonhole row work five 3ch loops, missing 3dc of previous row, at equal intervals along edge of 2nd row, then work a 4th row of dc, making 3dc into each buttonhole.

At lower edges of front borders, to match the fringes, take 1 strand of each colour and knot into fringes. Neaten all fringes with a sharp pair of scissors.

Attach 5 buttons to correspond with buttonholes.

For the draw-cord, using 3 strands of first colour, make

130ch. At neck-edge of garment weave remaining loops 3 × 3. Thread cord evenly through the woven loops. Make 2 tassels, or pom-poms, and attach to cord.

Bolero for a little girl

A bolero, easy to slip on and off, is a useful garment for people of all ages. This one, worked in three colours, is designed to fit a child from three to five years old, although it can easily be enlarged. Oddments of yarn may be used when available, but care must be taken that they are all of the same type and thickness.

MEASUREMENTS
To fit chest 45.6–56 cm (18–22 in.)
Length from top of shoulder to lower edge 31.5 cm (12.5 in.)

CHOICE OF YARN
Lee Target Supersoft Courtelle double knitting.

HOOK TEST
Note: When reference is made to the number of loops, this means the number of loops *on each prong.*
Using a hairpin size 6 cm (2.5 in.) and a No 4.00 hook, the test over 30 loops on 2 strips woven together was:
    5 loops = 2.5 cm (1 in.)
    Each strip when joined measured 4 cm (1.5 in.) wide.
    1 ball worked 222 loops.

PLANNING THE BOLERO
The bolero is made in three colours, woven together as shown in Fig. 34; 11 strips altogether. The numbers at the top of each strip indicate the colours, that is, 1, 2, and 3. The numbers at lower end of strips indicate the number of loops for that particular strip.
    It will be seen from the diagram that strips will be required as follows:

For the back
3 strips 1st Colour, each 48 loops
2 strips 2nd Colour, each 48 loops.

Underarms
2 strips 1st Colour, each 27 loops.

Fronts, shoulders, back
2 strips 2nd Colour, each 105 loops
2 strips 3rd Colour, each 105 loops

Fig. 34. The layout for the strips for the bolero.

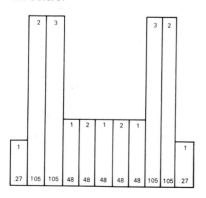

74

Edges

2 rows of dc will be made in 2nd Colour all round outer edges of bolero, giving a scalloped effect at lower and upper edges of strips.

YARN REQUIREMENT

1st Colour: 3 strips 48 loops each	144 loops
2 strips 27 loops each	54 loops
Total	198 loops

At 222 loops per ball, say 1 ball.

2nd Colour: 2 strips 48 loops each	96 loops
2 strips 105 loops each	210 loops
Total	306 loops

At 222 loops per ball, say 1·5 balls.

The 0·5 ball remaining will be used for the border.

3rd Colour: 2 strips 105 loops each	210 loops

At 222 loops per ball, say 1 ball.

TO MAKE THE BOLERO

Materials: 1st Colour 1 ball; 2nd Colour 2 balls; 3rd Colour 1 ball; Crochet hooks size 4·00 and 3·00; Hairpin 6 cm (2·5 in.).

Using the hairpin and No 4·00 hook, work all the strips as above.

Weaving 3 loops × 3 all the time, join strips as Fig. 34 indicates. Fasten off securely all final loops.

At armholes, weave 3 loops into 3, and fasten off.

For the edging, with No 3·00 hook, taking 3 loops together at fronts, work 2 rows dc evenly all round outer edges, fasten off.

Tunisian crochet

Tunisian crochet is worked with a long hook resembling a knitting needle, but with a hook at one end and a knob at the other to retain the stitches. Unlike the ordinary crochet hook, it has no flattened holding-point along the stem.

All Tunisian patterns are worked over two rows, the first from right to left picking up and retaining the loops or stitches, and the second from left to right to crochet the stitches off singly or in pattern, leaving at the top a row of chains. It is usual to begin working Tunisian with the first one or more rows in Tunisian simple, described on page 76. At the end of the work, one row of ordinary double-crochet stitches completes the final row.

Five different Tunisian patterns are described and pictured here. The designer will quickly be able to work out others in plain, or mixed colours.

The Tunisian topper (see plate 22) is a quick and easy example of pattern work done by this method.

For those who do not wish to design, the striped Tunic (see plate 31), with instructions on page 121, may prove a useful alternative.

TUNISIAN SIMPLE
This is shown in Fig. 35.
Begin with a chain of required length.
1st row Insert hook in 2nd ch from hook, * yoh and draw loop through, insert hook into next st, rep from * leaving all loops on hook.
Note: The work is *never* turned.
2nd row Yoh, and draw loop through, * yoh, draw through 2 loops, rep from * to end of row, 1ch.
Further rows Rep from 1st row, inserting hook under the vertical thread below, yoh, and draw loop through.

Fig. 35. Tunisian Simple.

CROSSED TUNISIAN
This is shown in Fig. 36.
Begin with 2 rows Tunisian Simple.
1st row 1ch, * insert hook from right to left under the *2nd* vertical thread, yoh, and draw loop through, rep through first (the one missed) vertical thread, rep from * to end.
2nd row As Tunisian Simple, after the first loop drawing through 3 loops to end of row.
Rep rows 1 and 2 as required.

Fig. 36. Crossed Tunisian.

TWO-COLOUR TUNISIAN
See plate 19.
This is worked as Tunisian Simple.
1st row First colour

76

2nd row Second colour
3rd row Second colour
4th row First colour
Rep 4 rows as required.

LACEY TUNISIAN
See plate 20.
1st row As Tunisian Simple
2nd row * 3ch, yoh and draw through 5 loops, yoh and draw through 1 loop. Rep from *, ending with 1ch.
3rd row Pick up loop at top of each cluster and 1 loop in each of 3ch, taking top thread of ch only, to end.
Rep rows 2 and 3 as required.

RIPPLE TUNISIAN IN TWO COLOURS
See plate 21.
Begin with 2 rows of Tunisian Simple.
1st row With first colour, insert hook into next vertical stitch, yoh and pull loop through (this is a knit-loop), make another knit-loop in next vertical stitch, slip hook through next two vertical stitches (these are slip-loops), 2 knit-loops, 4 half-closed tr (that is leaving last loops of each tr on hook), rep to end.
2nd row As 2nd row of Tunisian Simple.
3rd and 4th rows With second colour in Tunisian Simple.
5th row First colour, 1 knit-loop, * 4 half-closed tr, 2 knit-loops, 2 slip-loops, 2 knit-loops. Rep to end.
6th row As 2nd row Tunisian Simple.
7th and 8th rows Second colour, Tunisian Simple.
Rep rows 1 to 8 as required.
Note: Do not pull yarn too tightly at back of slip-loops.

Tunisian topper

This multi-coloured slip-over, shown in plate 22, with a square neck is made in two identical pieces. Although lacey in appearance, it is quick and easy to make. It can be worn as it is, or the square neck will complement any blouse underneath.

MEASUREMENTS
Bust—actual, without side lacings 40 cm (32 in.)
Length from shoulder, without fringe 50 cm (20 in.)

HOOK TEST
With No 4·00 Tunisian hook, worked over complete pattern.
Tension: 3 patterns (groups) = 5 cm (2 in.).

PATTERN
1 row Tunisian Simple
1 row 5-stitch groups

PLANNING THE GARMENT

The topper will have a series of contrasting colour stripes, as plate 22 shows. These can be made of oddments, or the quantities can be worked out on a group basis.

Every 2 rows will comprise 25 groups of 5 stitches each group. From the lower edge to the front neck there will be 44 pattern rows (88 rows total).

There are only two seams at top of each shoulder. The sides are joined with tassel-ended chain lacings, enabling the garment to be worn by a good range of sizes.

The coloured stripes are arranged as follows:

Main colour	(M)	First 16 pattern rows (32 rows)
1st Contrast	(C1)	Next 2 pattern rows (4 rows)
2nd Contrast	(C2)	Next 2 pattern rows (4 rows)
3rd Contrast	(C3)	Next 2 pattern rows (4 rows)
	C2	Next 2 pattern rows (4 rows)
	M	Next 2 pattern rows (4 rows)
	C2	Next 2 pattern rows (4 rows)
	C3	Next 2 pattern rows (4 rows)
	C2	Next 2 pattern rows (4 rows)
	C1	Next 2 pattern rows (4 rows)
	M	Next 2 pattern rows (4 rows)
	C1	Next 10 pattern rows (20 rows)
	C2	Next 10 pattern rows (20 rows)
	C3	Next 10 pattern rows (20 rows)
	C1	Next 2 pattern rows (4 rows)
	M	remainder, including shoulder straps

YARN REQUIREMENT

1 ball Main colour worked 16 pattern and 16 Tunisian Simple rows of 25 groups of 5 stitches each =	400 groups
Total number of M-colour groups to be worked back and front =	1598 groups
At 400 groups per ball =	say 4 balls
Fringes and lacings	say 1 ball
Total amount M	5 balls
Total number of C1 groups to be worked back and front = 450 groups	
At 400 groups per ball	say 2 balls
Total number of C2 groups to be worked, same as C1 =	450 groups
At 400 groups per ball	say 2 balls
Total number of C3 groups to be worked =	350 groups
At 400 groups per ball	say 1 ball

TO MAKE THE TOPPER

Materials: 5 balls Lee Target Duo double crêpe: Main Colour;
2 balls Lee Target Duo double crêpe: 1st Contrast; 2
balls Lee Target Duo double crêpe: 2nd Contrast; 1

ball Lee Target Duo double crêpe: 3rd Contrast; 1 Tunisian crochet hook No 4·00.

Note: The work should be held well down with the left hand, and the hook facing downwards, when the loops are being slipped off.

With No 4·00 Tunisian hook and M begin with 126ch.
1st row   (Tunisian Simple) Insert hook in 2nd ch from hook, yoh, then into each ch, to end. (126 loops.) Do not turn the work.
2nd row   (Pattern row) * 3ch, yoh, draw through 5 lps on hook, yoh, draw through 1 lp. Rep from * to last 2 lps, yoh, and draw through both lps. (25 groups.)
3rd row   Pick up one lp from last ch of previous row, 1 lp from each following group and 1 lp from each of 3ch, to end.
Rep 2nd and 3rd rows 36 times each to armhole, changing colours as indicated, or differently if preferred.
Rep 2nd row once more.

Armhole decrease
Ss over 3 gps, continue working row in pattern to last 3 gps unworked.
Next row   Continue in pattern for a further 13 rows to neck, ending with a pattern row.

Shoulder straps
Work in pattern over first 5 gps for 34 rows. Fasten off.
For second strap, leaving stitches for neck, rejoin yarn 5 complete groups in from end of row. Work in pattern over these for 34 rows. Fasten off.

Front
Work another piece exactly the same as back.

TO MAKE UP
Press both pieces lightly according to instructions. Join both shoulder seams.

The lacings
Using 2 strands of each of 4 colours, with No 4·00 hook work two lengths of chain each measuring approximately 100 cm (40 in.). Knot each end, and lace these at even intervals from the top of each side downwards. Tie in bows at base.

Fringes
Cut lengths of yarn 25 cm (10 in.) long, insert these at regular intervals along lower edge of garment, and knot. With a sharp pair of scissors neaten the fringes.

Part 2
A Miscellany of Patterns

Baby's matinée coat, bonnet, bootees and mittens

Crochet lends itself very well to baby wear, provided the pattern is not too open, otherwise tiny fingers may become entangled and frustrated baby cries are soon heard.

This ensemble (see plate 23) is pretty, quick and easy to make, and reasonably economical in yarn consumption.

MEASUREMENTS

To fit chest	45·5 cm (18 in.)	51 cm (20 in.)	56 cm (22 in.)
Length from top of shoulder	25·4 cm (10 in.)	27·9 cm (11 in.)	30·5 cm (12 in.)
Sleeve seam	12·7 cm (5 in.)	14 cm (5·5 in.)	15·2 cm (6 in.)

MATERIALS

Lee Target Lullaby Fairy Fondants double-knitting, as shown in plate 23, or Lee Target Cherub Baby Bri-nylon double-knitting.

Coat	5 balls	6 balls	7 balls
Bonnet	2 balls	3 balls	3 balls
Bootees	1 ball	1 ball	1 ball
Mittens	1 ball	1 ball	1 ball

Crochet hooks Nos 4·00 and 4·50
3 Buttons for coat
Ribbon for bonnet, bootees and mittens

Note: For 51 cm (20 in.) and 56 cm (22 in.) sizes, follow figures in parenthesis. When only one set of figures is given, the instruction applies to all sizes.

TENSION

4 hlf tr = 2·5 cm (1 in.)

COAT
Yoke
With No 4.00 hook, make 34(37; 40)ch.

1st row   1hlf tr in 2nd ch from hook, 1hlf tr in each rem ch, 1ch, turn, 33(36; 39)hlf tr.

2nd row   1hlf tr in each of next 2(1; 1)hlf tr, * 2hlf tr in next hlf tr, 1hlf tr in each of next 4hlf tr, rep from * to last 3(3; 2)hlf, tr, 2hlf tr in next hlf tr, 1hlf tr in each rem hlf tr, 1ch, turn. [41(45; 49)hlf tr.]

Work 4 more rows in this manner, working one more hlf tr between each inc on each row. [73(81; 89)hlf tr.]

7th and 8th rows   1hlf tr in each half tr, 1ch, turn.

9th row   1hlf tr in each of next 11(12; 13)hlf tr, miss next 14(16; 18)hlf tr 1hlf tr in each of next 23(25; 27)hlf tr, miss next 14(16; 18)hlf tr, 14(16; 18)ch, 1hlf tr in each rem 11(12; 13)hlf tr, 1ch, turn.

10th row   1hlf tr in each st to end, (i.e. 1hlf tr in each hlf tr, 1hlf tr in each ch), 1ch, turn. [73(81; 89)hlf tr.]

11th row   1hlf tr in each hlf tr to end, 1ch, turn.

Rep 11th row twice, no ch to turn after last row.

Using No 4.50 hook, proceed in skirt pattern.

1st row   (wrong side) 1dc in first hlf tr, * miss 1hlf tr, 3tr in next hlf tr, miss 1hlf tr, 1dc in next hlf tr, rep from * to end, 3ch, turn.

2nd row   * 2ch, 1dc in centre tr of block, 2ch, 1tr in next dc, rep from * to end, 2ch, turn.

3rd row   2tr in first tr, * 1dc in next dc, 5tr in next tr, rep from * ending last rep 3tr in 3rd of turning ch.

4th row   1dc in first tr, * 2ch, 1tr in next dc, 2ch, 1dc in next centre tr, rep from * ending last rep 2ch, 1dc in end tr.

5th row   1dc in first dc, * 5tr in next tr, 1dc in next dc, rep from * to end, 3ch, turn.

The 2nd to 5th rows (inclusive) form the pattern.

Continue in patt until coat measures 25.4 (27.9; 30.5)cm 10(11; 12)in. from shoulder, ending with a 5th row. Fasten off.

Sleeves
With No 4.00 hook and right side of coat facing, rejoin yarn and work 24(26; 28)hlf tr evenly across top of sleeve opening. Work 7.6 cm (3 in.) in hlf tr on these sts.

Next row   (right side facing) 1hlf tr in first hlf tr, dec 1, patt to last 3hlf tr, dec 1, 1hlf tr in end hlf tr, 1ch, turn.

Work 3 rows without shaping. Rep last 4 rows until 20hlf tr remain.

Continue without shaping until sleeve measures 16.5(17.8; 19)cm 6.5(7; 7.5)in. from beginning [first 5 cm (2 in.) of seam to sew to underarm of coat], ending with a right side row. Fasten off.

TO MAKE UP
Press each piece carefully according to instructions for yarn.

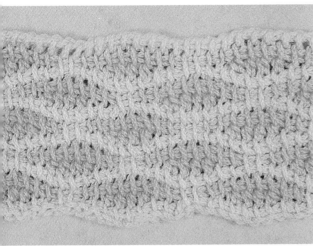

Plate 19 (*Top left*) Two-colour Tunisian.

Plate 20 (*Top right*) Lacey Tunisian.

Plate 21 (*Centre left*) Ripple Tunisian in two colours.

Plate 22 (*Above*) The Tunisian multi-coloured topper.

Plate 23 (*Left*) Baby's matinée coat, bonnet, bootees and mittens.

Plate 24 (*Top left*) Twins' dresses.
Plate 25 (*Top right*) The floppity
clown—make this from oddments from
the woolbag.
Plate 26 (*Above*) The Irish-crochet
blouse.
Plate 27 (*Right*) The skirt and
bolero—to suit any occasion.

Sew sleeve seams placing first 5 cm (2 in.) of underarm of coat.

Cuffs
With No 4·00 hook, wrong side of work facing, work 1 row of shell pattern round edge of sleeve, thus: 1dc in first hlf tr, * miss 1hlf tr, 5tr in next hlf tr, miss 1hlf tr, 1dc in next hlf tr, rep from * all round, ss to complete.
Fasten off.

Left front band
With right side of work facing, with No 4·00 hook, work 3 rows of hlf tr evenly up left front. Fasten off.

Right front band
With No 4·00 hook, with right side of work facing, work one row of hlf tr evenly up right front.
2nd row   (Buttonholes) 1hlf tr in first hlf tr, * miss 1hlf tr, 1ch, 1hlf tr in each of next 4hlf tr, rep from * twice, 1hlf tr in each hlf tr to end.
3rd row   1hlf tr in each hlf tr, working 1hlf tr in each buttonhole sp, do not break off yarn. Work one row dc evenly round neck edge. Fasten off.
Sew on buttons to correspond with buttonholes. Press seams.

BONNET
Using No 4·00 hook, make 3ch, 1ss into a circle.
1st round   8hlf tr into circle, 1ss to complete round, 1ch, turn.
2nd round   2hlf tr in each hlf tr to end, 1ss to complete round, 1ch, turn. (16hlf tr).
3rd round   * 2hlf tr in next hlf tr, 1hlf tr in next hlf tr, rep from * all round, 1ss to complete round, 1ch, turn. (24hlf tr.)
4th round   * 2hlf tr in next hlf tr, 1hlf tr in each of next 2hlf tr, rep from * all round, 1ss to complete round, 1ch, turn. (32hlf tr.)

45·5 cm (18 in.) size only
Next round   * 2hlf tr in next hlf tr, 1hlf tr in each of next 5hlf tr, rep from * 4 times more, 1hlf tr in each rem hlf tr. (37hlf tr.)

51 cm (20 in.) size only
Next round   * 2hlf tr in next hlf tr, 1hlf tr in each of next 3hlf tr, rep from * to last 4hlf tr, 2hlf tr in next hlf tr, 1hlf tr in each of next 2hlf tr, 2hlf tr in end hlf tr. (41hlf tr.)

56 cm (22 in.) size only
Next round   * 2hlf tr in next hlf tr, 1hlf tr in each of next 3hlf tr, rep from * to end. (40hlf tr.)

Next round   * 2hlf tr in next hlf tr, 1hlf tr in each of next 7hlf tr, rep from * to end (45hlf tr.)

All sizes with No 4·50 hook

1st row (wrong side) 1dc in first hlf tr, * miss 1hlf tr, 3tr in next hlf tr, miss 1hlf tr, 1dc in next hlf tr, rep from * to end, 3ch, turn.

2nd row * 2ch, 1dc in centre tr of block, 2ch, 1 tr in next dc, rep from * to end, 2ch, turn.

3rd row 2tr in first tr, * 1dc in next dc, 5tr in next tr, rep from * ending last rep 3tr in 3rd of turning ch.

4th row 1dc in first tr, * 2ch, 1tr in next dc, 2ch, 1dc in next centre tr, rep from * ending last rep 2ch, 1dc in end tr.

5th row 1dc in first dc, * 5tr in next tr, 1dc in next dc, rep from * to end, 3ch, turn.

Rep 2nd to 5th rows twice, then 2nd and 3rd rows again, 1ch, turn.

Next row Working into front loop of tr only, 1hlf tr in each of 3tr, * miss 1dc, 1hlf tr in each of 4tr, rep from * to last 3tr, 1hlf tr in each of 3tr. Fasten off.

TO MAKE UP

Pin out and press as yarn instructions. Sew back seam 2·5 cm (1 in.) from crown. Fold front edge back at first row of shells.

With No 4·00 hook, work one row dc round neck edge. Sew on ribbon.

BOOTEES

With No 4·00 hook, make 7ch.

1st row 1hlf tr in 2nd ch from hook, 1hlf tr in each rem ch, 1ch, turn (6hlf tr).

2nd row 1hlf tr in each hlf tr to end, 1ch, turn.

Rep 2nd row 6(8; 10) times.

Proceed as follows:

1st round 1hlf tr in each hlf tr to end, do not turn, work 12(14; 16)hlf tr along side edge, 6hlf tr along lower edge, 12(14; 16)hlf tr along other side edge, ss to complete round, 1ch, turn. 36(40; 44)hlf tr.

2nd round Dec 1, 1hlf tr in each of next 8(10; 12)hlf tr, dec 1, 1hlf tr in each of next 6hlf tr, dec 1, 1hlf tr in each of next 8(10; 12)hlf tr, dec 1, 1hlf tr in each of next 6hlf tr, ss to complete round, 1ch, turn. 32(36; 40)hlf tr.

3rd round 1hlf tr in each hlf tr to end, ss to complete round, 1ch, turn. Rep 3rd round once.

Next row 1hlf tr in each of 6hlf tr, 1ch, turn.

Work 4 more rows on these 6hlf tr.

Next round Miss 6hlf tr of main part, 1hlf tr in each of next 14(18; 22)hlf tr, ss to complete round, 1ch, turn.

Next round * Miss 1hlf tr, 1ch, 1hlf tr in next hlf tr, rep from * all round, ss to complete, 1ch, turn.

Next round * 1hlf tr in next hlf tr, 1hlf tr in next ch sp, rep from * all round, ss to complete, 1ch, turn.

Work one more round in hlf tr on these sts.

Work one row in shell patt. Fasten off.

TO MAKE UP
Pin out and press. Sew up front seams. Thread ribbon through holes.

MITTENS
With No 4·00 hook, make 3ch, ss into circle.
1st round   8hlf tr into circle, ss to complete round, 1ch, turn.
2nd round   2hlf tr into first hlf tr, 1hlf tr in each of next 2hlf tr, 2hlf tr in each of next 2hlf tr, 1hlf tr in each of next 2hlf tr, 2hlf tr in last hlf tr, ss to complete round, 1ch, turn. (12 hlf tr.)
3rd round   1hlf tr in each hlf tr, ss to complete round, 1ch, turn.
4th round   2hlf tr in first hlf tr, 1hlf tr in each of next 4hlf tr, 2hlf tr in each of next 2hlf tr, 1hlf tr in each of next 4hlf tr, 2hlf tr in last hlf tr, ss to complete round, 1ch, turn. (16hlf tr.)

51 and 56 cm (20 and 22 in.) sizes only
Next round   As 3rd round.
Next round   2hlf tr in first hlf tr, 1hlf tr in each of next 6hlf tr, 2hlf tr in each of next 2hlf tr, 1hlf tr in each of next 6hlf tr, 2hlf tr in last hlf tr. (20hlf tr.)

56 cm (22 in.) size only
Next round   As 3rd round.
Next round   2hlf tr in first hlf tr, 1hlf tr in each of next 8hlf tr, 2hlf tr in each of next 2hlf tr, 1hlf tr in each of next 8hlf tr, 2hlf tr in last hlf tr. (24hlf tr.)

All sizes
Rep 3rd round until work measures 6·3(7·6; 9)cm/2·5(3; 3·5)in. from beginning.
Next round   (right side facing) * Miss 1hlf tr, 1ch, 1hlf tr in next hlf tr, rep from * all round, ss to complete round, 1ch, turn.
Next round   1hlf tr in each st, ss to complete round, 1ch, turn. Rep 3rd round once.
Next round   Work in shell patt. Fasten off.
Thread ribbon through holes at wrist.

Twins—but not identical

The two dresses, shown in plate 24, are good examples of plain and lacey garments. While one is excellent for daytime rough-and-tumble wear, the other, worked in a sparkling yarn, would enhance any little girl's social occasion.

TO MAKE THE PLAIN DRESS
Measurements:
Chest   56·5 cm/(22 in.)   61 cm/(24 in.)   66 cm/(26 in.)

71 cm/(28 in.)
Length from top of shoulder (adjustable)
40·5 cm/(16 in.)   44·5 cm/(17·5 in.)   48 cm/(19 in.)
55·5 cm/22 in.)
Sleeve seam 5 cm/(2 in.) 5 cm/(2 in.) 6 cm/(2·5 in.) 7·5 cm/(3 in.)
Materials: Motoravia double-knitting—10; 11; 12; 13 balls;
    Crochet hooks Nos 3·50 and 3·00 (for all sizes); But-
    tons—4 (for all sizes); One 10-cm zip fastener (all
    sizes).
Tension: With 3·50 hook 9dc = 5 cm (2 in.)

Note: The first set of figures is for 56·5 cm (22 in.) chest, the first
bracketed set is for 61 cm (24 in.) chest, the second bracketed set
is for 66 cm (26 in.) chest, and the third bracketed set is for
71 cm (28 in.) chest.

Abbreviations: Complete list appears on page 13.

Note: The dress is worked from shoulder to hem.

Front—right shoulder
With No 3·50 hook, make 12(13; 14; 15)ch.
1st row   1dc in 2nd ch from hook, 1dc in each rem ch, 11(12;
13; 14)dc, turn.
2nd row   1dc in each dc to last dc, 2dc in end dc, turn.
3rd row   1dc in each dc to end, turn.
Rep 2nd and 3rd rows once, then 2nd row once. 14(15; 16;
17)dc.
7th row   2dc in first dc, 1dc in each rem dc, turn.
8th row   As 2nd row, 16(17; 18; 19)dc. Fasten off.

Front—left shoulder
Using No 3·50 hook, make 12(13; 14; 15)ch.
1st row   1dc in 2nd ch from hook, 1dc in each rem ch. 11(12;
13; 14)dc, turn.
2nd row   2dc in first dc, 1dc in each rem dc, turn.
3rd row   1dc in each dc to end.
Rep 2nd and 3rd rows once, then 2nd row once. 14(15; 16;
17)dc.
7th row   1dc in each dc to last dc, 2dc in end dc, turn.
8th row   As 2nd row.
9th row   1dc in each dc to end, make 10(12; 14; 16)ch, then
beginning at shaped edge of right shoulder piece, work 1dc in
each dc.
10th row   1dc in each dc to centre 10(12; 14; 16)ch, 1dc in each
dc to end.
11th row   1dc in each dc to end. 42(46; 50; 54)dc.
The 11th row forms the patt. Work 4(4; 6; 8) rows in patt.

Shape armholes
Next row   2dc in first dc, patt to last dec, 2dc in end dc.
Next row   Patt to end.

Rep last 2 rows once, making 4ch at end of last row.

Next row   Miss first ch, 1dc in each of foll 3ch, dc to end, make 4ch.

Next row   Miss first ch, 1dc in each of foll 3ch, dc to end. 52(56; 60; 64)dc.

Work 6(8; 10, 12) rows in patt without shaping.

Shape skirt

1st row   1dc in each of first 7(8; 9; 10)dc, 2dc in next dc (inc made), 1dc in next dc, 2dc in next dc (inc made), 1dc in each of foll 32(34; 36; 38)dc, inc in next dc, 1dc in next dc, inc in next dc, 1dc in each rem dc. [56(60; 64; 68)dc.]

Work 7(9; 11; 13) rows in patt without shaping.

Next row   1dc in each of first 7(8; 9; 10)dc, inc in next dc, 1dc in each of next 3dc, inc in next dc, 1dc in each of foll 32(34; 36; 38)dc, inc in next dc, 1dc in each of next 3dc, inc in next dc, 1dc in each rem dc. [60(64; 68; 72)dc.]

Cont in patt inc 4sts on every foll 8(10; 12; 14)th row (working the extra sts between the 2 inc sts as before) until 6 inc rows have been worked in all. [76(80; 84; 88)dc.]

Cont in patt without further shaping until work measures 40·5 cm (44·5; 48·25; 55·5)cm, 16(17·5; 19; 22)in. (or desired length) from beginning. Fasten off.

Back—left side

Work 1st to 4th rows (inclusive) as given for front right side, making 9(10; 11; 12)ch at end of last row.

Next row   Miss first ch, 1dc in each foll ch, 1dc in each rem dc. [21(23; 25; 27)dc.]

Continue without shaping until work measures same as front to first armhole shaping. Shape armhole to correspond with front, ending on right side.

Back—right side

Work 1st to 3rd rows (inclusive) as given for front left side. Fasten off.

Make 8(9; 10; 11)ch, and working across 12(13; 14; 15)dc just worked.

Next row   Patt to last 8(9; 10; 11)ch, 1dc in each ch. [21(23; 25; 27)dc.]

Continue in patt until work measures same as front to first armhole shaping.

Shape armhole to correspond with front, ending on wrong side, then, beg at inside edge, patt across left side, 52(56; 60; 64)dc. Complete to correspond with front.

Sleeves

With No 3·50 hook, make 9ch.

1st row   1dc in 2nd ch, 1dc in each foll ch, make 3ch.

2nd row   Miss first ch, 1dc in each foll ch, patt to end, make

3ch.

Rep 2nd row twice.

5th row   Miss first dc, 1dc in each foll dc, patt to end.

6th row   2dc in first dc (inc made), dc to last dc, 2dc in end dc. Increase once at each end of every foll alt row until there are 24(26; 28; 30)dc.

Next row   Patt to end, make 4ch.

Next row   Miss first ch, 1dc in each foll ch, patt to end, make 4ch.

Next row   Miss first ch, 1dc in each foll ch, patt to end. 30(32; 34; 36)dc.

Work 2(2; 4; 6) rows in patt.

1st row   Miss first dc, patt to last 2dc, miss next dc, 1dc in end dc.

Work 3 rows in patt, then 1st row once more. Fasten off.

Mock pocket pieces (2)

Using No 3·00 hook, make 14(15; 16; 17)ch.

1st row   1dc in 2nd ch, 1dc in each foll ch.

2nd row   1dc in each dc to end.

Rep 2nd row twice, do not turn work, cont in dc round outer edge, working 2dc in each corner, 1dc in side edges and 1dc in each dc on two other edges.

Shoulder pieces (2)

Using No 3·50 hook, make 11(12; 13; 14)ch.

1st row   1dc in 2nd ch, 1dc in each foll ch, cont in dc all round, working 2dc in each corner. Fasten off.

Sew up shoulder seams.

Neckband

With right side facing, with No 3·00 hook, beg at left back opening, work 6(6; 8; 8) rows in dc evenly round neck edge. Fasten off.

TO MAKE UP

Following yarn instructions, press carefully. Sew in sleeves. Sew up side and sleeve seams. Sew pocket pieces in position across upper edge only and sew button at centre of each flap. Place shoulder pieces across shoulder seam and sew down at each end. Sew button at outside edge. Sew in zip fastener. Press all seams.

TO MAKE THE LACEY DRESS

This dress, with plain yoke and front opening features a shell-pattern skirt.

Materials: 7 balls Lister Bel Air Starspun; 1 No 3·50 crochet hook; 2 buttons.

Measurements:

To fit chest 43 cm–53 cm (17–21 in.)

Length from shoulder 38 cm (15 in.); adjustable.
Tension: 5tr = 2·5 cm (1 in.) with No 3·50 hook.

Note: A V-stitch is worked by making 1tr, 1ch, 1tr into the same st. A shell is worked by making 3tr, 1ch, 3tr, into same st. A picot is worked by making 1dc, 3ch, 1dc into same st.

The yoke
This begins at neck edge, with 69ch.
1st row   1tr in 4th ch from hook, 1tr in each of next 12ch, 3tr into next ch, 1tr into each of next 5ch, 3tr into next ch, 1tr into each of next 25ch, 3tr into next ch, 1tr into each of next 5ch, 3tr into next ch, 1tr into each rem 14ch, turn.
2nd row   3ch, miss first tr, 1tr into each of next 14tr, 3tr into next tr, 1tr into each of next 7tr, 3tr into next tr, 1tr into each of next 27tr, 3tr into next tr, 1tr into each of next 7tr, 3tr into next tr, 1tr into each of next 14tr, 1tr into top of 3ch, turn.
3rd row   3ch, miss first tr, 1tr in each of next 15tr, 3tr into next tr, 1tr into each of next 9tr, 3tr in next tr, 1tr in each of next 29tr, 3tr into next tr, 1tr in each of next 9tr, 3tr in next tr, 1tr in each of next 15tr, 1tr in top of 3ch, turn.
4th row   3ch, miss first tr, 1tr in each of next 16tr, 3tr in next tr, 1tr in each of next 11tr, 3tr in next tr, 1tr in each of next 31tr, 3tr in next tr, 1tr in each of next 11tr, 3tr in next tr, 1tr in each of next 16tr, 1tr in top of 3ch turn.
5th row   3ch, miss first tr, 1tr in each of next 17tr, 3tr in next tr, 1tr in each of next 13tr, 3tr in next tr, 1tr in each of next 33tr, 3tr in next tr, 1tr in each of next 13tr, 3tr in next tr, 1tr in each of next 17tr, 1tr in top of 3ch, turn.
6th row   3ch miss first tr, 1tr in each of next 18tr, 3tr in next tr, 1tr in each of next 15tr, 3tr in next tr, 1tr in each of next 35tr, 3tr in next tr, 1tr in each of next 15tr, 3tr in next tr, 1tr in each of next 18tr, 1tr in top of 3ch, turn.
With a small safety pin, or other marker, mark the first tr of first 3tr gp, and last tr of last 3tr gp.
Fold the yoke so that the front edges overlap 2sts at centre, and catch stitch in position at lower edge.

The front
Join yarn to first marked tr of yoke and continue:
1st row   4ch, miss 1tr, 1tr into next tr, (1ch, miss 1tr, 1tr in next tr) 17 times, working last tr into 2nd marked tr of yoke, turn.
2nd row   3ch, (3tr in next sp, 1tr in next tr) 17 times, 3tr in next sp, 1tr in 3rd of 4ch, turn.
3rd row   3ch, 2tr in first tr, miss 2tr, V-st in next tr, (miss 2tr, shell in next tr, miss 2tr, V-st in next tr) 11 times, miss 2tr, 3tr in top of 3ch, turn.
4th row   3ch, shell into next V-st, (V-st into next sh, sh into next V-st) 11 times, 1tr into top of 3ch, turn.
5th row   3ch, 2tr in first tr, V-st in next sh, (sh into next V-st, V-

st into next sh) 11 times, 3tr in top of 3ch, turn.
Mark each end of last row.
Cont rep rows 4 and 5 until work measures 36·5 cm (14·5 in.) or desired length. Fasten off.

The back
Join yarn to first marked tr of yoke, and rep as for front.

The sleeves (both alike)
With right side of work facing, join yarn to side seam at underarm, 3ch, work 13tr along row ends up to yoke, 1tr in each of 19tr of yoke, 13tr down to side seam, 1ss into top of 3ch, turn.
Next row   3ch, 1tr into each tr to end, 1ss in top of 3ch.
Now work in *rounds*:
1st round   1dc in every tr to end.
2nd round   * Miss next dc, 1dc in each of next 3dc, rep from * to end.
3rd round   1dc in every dc to end, 1ss into first dc. Fasten off.

Neck edging
With right side facing, join yarn to neck at left side of front opening, work a picot into same st, * miss 1st, pct into next st, rep from * to end.

Lower edging
With right side facing, join yarn to first tr at one side, into same tr work 1 pct, (miss 1 tr, 1 pct in next tr) rep all round edge, join with 1ss.

To complete
Work 1 row dc evenly along left side of front opening. Work 1 row dc evenly along right side of front opening, making two 2dc buttonholes. A ribbon tie round neck may be added, with bow at the front.

Popette the poodle

Loop stitch gives a lifelike look of the softest texture to this very attractive toy (see Fig. 37). It is washable and very durable, and any small child would welcome it into the home.

MATERIALS
9 balls Lister Lavenda double crêpe, or Lavenda double-knitting; Crochet hook No 3·00; Non-flammable, washable stuffing.

MEASUREMENT
Top of head to feet = 25·25 cm (10 in.)

Fig. 37. Loop stitch for Popette the poodle.

TO WORK LOOP STITCH (lp st)
With wrong side facing, wrap yarn once completely round first finger of left hand, keeping finger as close to work as possible. Insert hook in next stitch, then insert it from left to right under the 2 strands of yarn on the finger. Draw all through first loop on hook, yoh and draw through all 3 loops on hook.

TO MAKE THE POODLE
Body
Begin at centre chest, 4ch, join with 1ss to form a ring.
1st round   Work 6dc in ring.
2nd round   Inc 6dc in ring (12dc).
Next 4 rounds   Inc 6sts on each round (36dc).
Put a marker of contrast yarn, or small safety pin, here and work until the pieces measure 20·25 cm (8 in.) from the mark. Stuff body here.
Next 5 rounds   Dec 6sts on each round, stuffing as you go (6dc).
Now dec 3sts. Finish off and pull tight.

Legs (4)
Begin at foot and work as for body in dc for 3 rounds (18dc). Work without inc for 6 rounds. Change to lp st. Work 3 rounds. Inc 3 sts on next round (21sts). Work 3 rounds. Inc 4sts on next round (25sts). Work 3 rounds. Inc 5sts on next round. Work 3 rounds. Inc 5 sts on next round. Work 3 rounds. Inc 5sts on next round. Work 3 rounds. (35sts.)

Flap for shoulder
Work 17 lp sts, 1ch, turn.
1dc in each on next 17sts, 1ch, turn.
Rep last 2 rows 4 times more, then 1 row of lp st. Break off. Make 3 more legs.
Place a circle of cardboard about 2·5 cm (1 in.) across each foot, stuff, and sew to body, stuffing shoulder flaps as you go.

Head
Begin at top of head, work as for body for one round.

Change to lp st and shape as for body by inc 6sts every round for 8 rounds. (54sts.)
Dec 2 lp sts on next round, then dec 4sts on each of next 3 rounds. (40sts.)
Continue working in dc only. Dec 2sts on each of next 5 rounds. (30sts.) Then work straight for 16 rounds more. Break off and stuff.

Face
Begin at centre of face and work as for body in dc for 4 rounds. (24dc.) Work straight for 8 rounds (inc 3dc in next round, work 2 rounds) twice. (30dc.) Finish off and stuff. Sew onto head.

Tail
Begin at top of tail and work as for head in lp st for 3 rounds (18sts). Work one round. Now change to dc, dec 4sts on next round (14dc.) Work 10 rounds straight. Break off. Sew to body.

Ears (2)
Begin at lower edge with 16ch.
1st row Work lp st in 2nd ch from hook, and each ch to end, 1ch, turn.
2nd row 1dc in each st.
3rd row 1 lp st in each st, 1ch, turn.
4th row Miss 1st dc, work to within 1dc of end, 1ch, turn.
5th row Rep 3rd row.
Now work 2nd to 5th rows four times more (5 lp sts).
Next row 1dc in each of 5sts.
Finish off, and sew onto head.

To complete
Attach bow of ribbon.

Everyone loves a clown

Printed by kind permission of *Woman's Weekly*.
Children and adults alike are sure to fall for this enchanting floppy toy. He is very simple to make—just circular motifs strung together on elastic. Economical too, for he can be made with oddments from the wool bag. (See plate 25.)

MATERIALS
About 0·5 of a ball of 4-ply yarn in each of three colours; A small quantity of white for the head; Red and black yarn for embroidering the features; Crochet hooks size 4·00 and 2·50; Three 1·25 cm (0·5 in.) circles of red felt; 4 kitten bells; 1·8 m (2 yds) of roll elastic.

TENSION
1 large motif = 5 cm (2 in.) across

1 small motif = 4 cm (1·75 in.) across.

MEASUREMENT
To top of hat = 30 cm (10 in.)

TO MAKE THE CLOWN

Large motif
Make 4 in each of 3 colours for body, and the same for each leg.
With No 4·00 hook, make 4ch, join into ring with 1ss.
1st round   2ch, 9dc into ring, join with 1ss.
2nd round   5ch, 1tr in same place as join, (2ch, 1tr) twice into each dc, 2ch, join to 3rd of 5ch. Fasten off.

Small motif
Make 3 in each of 3 colours for each arm.
With No 2·50 hook work as for large motif, but work only 8dc instead of 9 into ring in first round.

The head
With No 4·00 hook and white yarn double, make 4ch, join into ring with 1ss.
1st round   2ch for first dc, 11dc into ring, joint with 1ss to 2ch at beg. (12dc.)
2nd round   2ch for first dc, 1dc in same place, 2dc in each of rem 11dc, join with 1ss. (24dc.)
Working 2ch for first dc in each round continue as follows:
Next round   Inc in every 3rd dc. (32dc.)
Work 9 rounds of dc over dc.
Next round   Dec by missing every 4th dc. (24dc.)
Work 1 round of dc over dc.
Next round   Miss every 3rd dc.
Break off yarn. Stuff head
Run end of yarn through last row of dc, draw up, and fasten off securely.

The hat
With No 4·00 hook, using first colour double, make 4ch, join into ring with 1ss.
1st round   2ch, 7dc into ring, join with 1ss.
2nd round   2ch for first dc, 1dc into each dc, join with 1ss.
Working 2ch for first dc in each round, continue as follows:
3rd round   Inc in alternate dc. (12dc.)
4th round   Inc in every 3rd dc. (16dc.)
5th round   Inc in every 4th dc. (20dc.)
6th round   Dc over dc.
7th round   Inc in every 5th dc. (24dc.)
8th round   Dc over dc.
9th round   Inc in every 4th dc. (30dc.)
10th and 11th rounds   Dc over dc.

Break off yarn, turn, join in second colour and using yarn double, work 3 rounds dc, join with 1ss, and fasten off.

TO MAKE UP
Tie a bell in centre of a 68·5 cm (27 in.) length of elastic, then thread both ends up through 12 leg motifs, alternating the colours. Repeat with other leg motifs, then thread all four strands of elastic up through body motifs, arranging them in the same order. Now take up ends through head and, drawing them up to measure about 23 cm (9 in.) from end of legs, tie off securely.

For arms, tie a bell about 23 cm (9 in.) from end of remaining elastic, take both ends through 9 arm motifs, then take long end through other arm motifs. Tie on a bell so that arms measure about 15 cm (6 in.) right across, return elastic through one arm, then tie ends round body elastic between 2nd and 3rd motifs from neck.

Embroider face as shown in plate 25, placing eyes about halfway down. Stitch hat to head, turning up brim.

Lucky the Lamb

This cuddly little lamb (see Fig. 38) would be the dearest pet of any small child. The loop stitch of which it is composed is quite easy to work, and makes the toy extra soft in texture.

MATERIALS
8 balls Lister Lavenda double crêpe in a light shade; 1 ball Lister Lavenda double crêpe in a dark shade; Crochet hook No 3·00; Kapok, wool cuttings, or other non-flammable stuffing; Felt for eyes and nose; Ribbon for neck.

MEASUREMENT
Length from top of head to feet 28 cm (11 in.).

TENSION
4·5sts = 2·5 cm (1 in.)

TO WORK LOOP STITCH (lp st)
With wrong side facing, wrap wool once completely round first finger on left hand. Keeping finger as near to work as possible, insert hook in next stitch, then insert it from left to right under the 2 strands of wool on the finger. Draw all through first loop on hook, wool over hook and draw through all 3 loops on hook.

TO MAKE THE LAMB
Body
Begin at centre front, using Main (M) colour, with No 3·00 hook

Fig. 38. Lucky the lamb.

ch 4, join with 1ss to form a circle. Work 6dc in circle. Now work in loop stitch.

Next round   Increase in each st. (12 lp sts.)

Next 4 rounds   Inc 6sts on each of these rounds. (36sts.)
Continue on these sts until work measures 20·25 cm (8 in.) from last row. Stuff well but not too firmly.

Next 5 rounds   Dec 6sts on each of these rounds, stuffing as work proceeds. (6sts.)
Dec 3sts. Break off, pull tight, and finish off.

Legs (4)

Starting at foot, with dark contrast (C) yarn and No 3·00 hook, join 4ch with 1ss to form a circle, and work 6dc in circle.

Next round   Inc in each st. (12sts.)

Next round   Inc 6sts (i.e. 1 on each alt st). (18 sts.)

Next 6 rounds   Work plain on 18sts. Fasten off.
Change to M, and work in lp st for 14 rounds.

Shoulder shaping

Work 12 lp sts, 1ch, turn.

2nd row   Work 12dc into loop sts, turn.
Rep last 2 rows once more, then first row once more. Fasten off.
Put circles of cardboard the size of 2·5 cm (1 in.) diameter in foot, stuff leg and sew to body, stuffing shoulder as you go.

Head

Beginning at crown, using M and 3·00 hook, 4ch, join with 1ss to form circle, work 6dc into circle. Now work in loop st.
2nd round Inc in each st (12 lps).
Now inc 6sts on each of next 5 rounds (42sts).
Continue on these sts until work measures 10 cm (4 in.).
Now dec 3sts on every round until 7sts remain. Fasten off. Stuff, and attach to body.

Tail

Using No 3·00 crochet hook and M, make 4ch, join with 1ss to form a circle. Work 6dc into circle now work in lp st.
2nd round Inc in each st. (12 lps.)
Continue on these sts until work measures 5 cm (2 in.). Fasten off. Attach to body.

Ears (2)

Using No 3·00 hook and M, make 12ch, and work one row in dc, then one row in lp st. Rep last 2 rows until work measures 5 cm (2 in.). Now dec one st at each end of next and foll alt rows until 3sts remain. Fasten off. Attach ears to head as illustrated in Fig. 38.

Nose

With No 3·00 hook and C, make 3ch, join with 1ss to form circle. 5dc into circle.
2nd round 2dc into each dc of previous round. (10dc.)
3rd round 1dc into each dc of previous round.
4th round 2dc into each dc of previous round. (20dc.)
5th round 1dc into each dc of previous round.
6th round 2dc into each alt dc of previous round. (30dc.)
7th round 1dc into each dc of previous round.
8th round 1dc into each dc of previous round.
9th round 1dc into each of next 20dc, turn.
10th round 1dc into each of last 20dc.
Now dec one st at each end of every row until 4dc remain. Fasten off. Stuff nose and attach to head.
Cut 2 circles of felt and stick, or sew to head for eyes, and one circle for nose, as shown in Fig. 38.
Tie ribbon round neck.

Flower-motif bikini

Printed by kind permission of Susan Shanks & Partners, Holborn, London WC1V 7DX. The bikini shown in Fig. 39.

MATERIALS
5 (6) balls Jewel yarn (Abbeydale).
182 cm (2 yds) elastic 1·25 cm (0·5 in.) wide

14 small round buttons or beads
No 3·50 crochet hook for 91 cm (36 in.) size
No 3·00 crochet hook for 86·25 cm (34 in.) size

TENSION
With No 3·50 hook 5 hlf tr = 2·5 cm (1 in.)

SIZES
To make the 86·25 cm (34 in.) size use hook No 3·00
To make the 91·0 cm (36 in.) size use hook No 3·50

TO MAKE THE BIKINI
Pants
Beginning at front, with No 3·00 hook make 72ch (loosely).
1st row   1hlf tr in 3rd ch from hook, 1hlf tr in each ch to end of row, 2ch, turn.

Fig. 39. The flower-motif bikini.

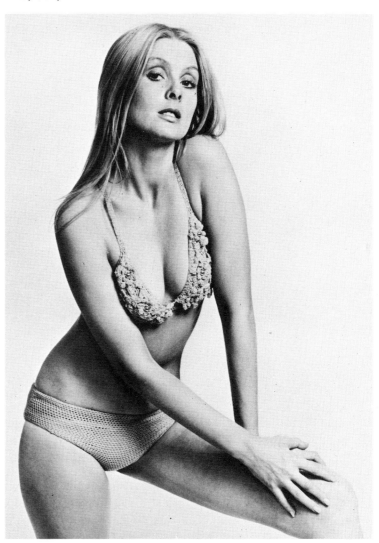

2nd row 1hlf tr in 2nd st, 1hlf tr in each st to end of row, 2ch, turn.

Rep last row 12 times.

15th row Ss over 10sts, 1hlf tr in each st to last 10sts, turn.

16th row Ss 2sts, 1hlf tr in each st to last 2sts, turn.

Rep last row twice.

19th row 1hlf tr in 2nd st, 1hlf tr in each st, till 2 rem, miss next st, 1hlf tr in last st, 2ch, turn.

Rep this last row until there are 14hlf tr across row, counting the 2ch as 1hlf tr.

Work straight for 7·5 cm (3 in.).

Next row Inc in first and last st.

Next row Work straight.

Rep last 2 rows 5 times, then inc at each end of every row until there are 70hlf tr across row.

Work 14 rows straight.

Next row Ss over 9sts, 1hlf tr in each st to last 9sts, turn.

Rep last row twice. Fasten off.

Join side seams and work 1 row of hlf tr round waist edge, then, using No 3·00 hook, work 2 rows of dc round each leg.

Note: Size 3·00 hook is used for this in both sizes.

Make a small turning at waist, stitch in herringbone stitch to allow for stretching, and insert required length of elastic.

Bra

With No 3·00 hook, make 133ch (loosely).

1st row 1hlf tr in 3rd ch from hook, 1hlf tr in each ch to end, 2ch, turn.

2nd row 1hlf tr in each st to end of row, 2ch, turn.

Rep last row twice, then begin to shape cups.

1st row Ss over 33sts, 2ch, 1hlf tr in next 33sts, turn, and work on this section only.

2nd row 1hlf tr in 2nd st, 1hlf tr in next 3sts, * 2hlf tr in next st, 1hlf tr in next 4sts. Rep from * to end of row, 2ch, turn.

3rd row 1hlf tr in each st to end of row, 2ch, turn.

4th row 1hlf tr in 2nd st, 1hlf tr in next 6sts, 2hlf tr in next st, * (1hlf tr in next 4sts, 2hlf tr in next st) 3 times, 1hlf tr in each st to end of row, 2ch, turn.

5th row 1hlf tr in 2nd st. 1hlf tr in each st to last 2sts, miss next st, 1hlf tr in last st, 2ch, turn.

Rep last row 4 times.

10th row 1hlf tr in 2nd st, 1hlf tr in each st to end of row, 2ch, turn.

11th row 1hlf tr in each st to end of row, 2ch, turn.

12th row 1hlf tr in 2nd st, 1hlf tr in each st to end of row, 2ch, turn.

Rep last row three times.

16th row As 5th row.

Rep last row until row reading 1hlf tr in 2nd st, 1hlf tr in next

2sts has been worked (4sts). Fasten off.

Join yarn at centre of bra, and work the other cup, but reverse all shapings.

Work 1 row in dc round top edge of bra, 2ch, turn.

Next row   1dc in first 33dc, * 1dc in next 6dc, miss 1dc. Rep from * to last 33sts, 1dc in each st to end, 2ch, turn.

Rep last row once.

Make a small turning at lower edge of bra, and insert required length of elastic, sufficient to give a snug fit when slightly stretched. If necessary a length of Shirlastic can be threaded round outer edge of bra cup to give a tighter fit.

Motif (make 12)

With No 3·00 hook, make 5ch, join into ring with 1ss.

1st round   2ch, 11hlf tr into ring, 1ss into top of 2ch.

2nd round   * (1dc, 1hlf tr, 1tr, 1dbl tr, 1tr, 1hlf tr, 1dc) in first sp, 1dc in next sp. Rep from * to end of round. (6 petals.)

3rd round   * 4ch, 1dc in dc after first petal. Rep from * to end of round, turn.

4th round   * (1dc, 1hlf tr, 3tr, 3dbl tr, 3tr, 1hlf tr, 1dc) in first ch lp. Rep from * in each lp to end of round.

Fasten off.

Join six motifs at petal tips to form a triangle thus:

Place triangle on bra cup and stitch in place.

Sew a round button, or bead, in centre of each motif.

Make another triangle with remaining 6 motifs and stitch to other bra cup.

Sew 2 buttons at edge of back fastening, and make 2 ch lps for corresponding buttonholes on other side.

With No 3·00 hook join yarn and work 4hlf tr across centre top of bra cup. Continue on these 4sts until strap measures 38 cm (15 in.). Fasten off. Make second strap to match. Sew both straps in place at back of bra.

Irish-crochet blouse

Printed by kind permission of J. & P. Coats (UK) Ltd, Glasgow.

This charming blouse (see Fig. 40 and plate 26) was modelled in one of Associated Television's *Women Today* Crochet Parties, and received much acclaim from the viewing public, including a celebrated actress and authoress. It is made in a style which will not date as time goes by, and its length can easily be adjusted. As cotton is used it does take considerably longer to make than its counterparts in thicker yarns, but the result cannot be compared for daintiness, laundering, and near-everlasting wear.

MATERIALS

Coats Mercer Crochet No 20 (20 gm)—16 balls for first size, 16 for second, and 17 for third size; Steel crochet hook No 1·25; 9 buttons.

Fig. 40. The lacey pattern for the Irish-crochet blouse.

To fit bust size	86·5 cm	91·5 cm	96·5 cm
	(34 in.)	(36 in.)	(38 in.)
Length from centre back	48 cm	48·5 cm	49 cm
	(19 in.)	(19·25 in.)	(19·5 in.)
Length of sleeve seam all sizes	45·5 cm	45·5 cm	45·5 cm
	(18 in.)	(18 in.)	(18 in.)

Note: Sizes in brackets refer to larger sizes. Where only one figure is given this refers to all sizes.

LAUNDERING THE BLOUSE

Use a warm lather of pure soap flakes and wash in the usual way, either by hand or washing machine. If desired, the blouse may be spin-dried until it is damp, or left until it is half dry.

Place a piece of paper, either plain white or squared on top of a clean, flat board. Following the correct measurements, draw the shape of the finished article on to the paper, using ruler and set square for squares and rectangles and a pair of compasses for circles. Using rustless pins, pin the crochet out to the pencilled shape, taking care not to strain the crochet. Pin out the general shape first, then finish by pinning out each picot, loop or space into position. Special points to note carefully when pinning out are:

1. When pinning loops, make sure the pin is in the centre of each loop to form balanced lines.

2. When pinning scallops, make all the scallops the same size and regularly curved.

3. Pull out all picots.

4. Where there are flowers, pull out each petal in position.

5. When pinning filet crochet, make sure that the spaces and blocks are square and that all edges are even and straight.

If the crochet requires to be slightly stiffened, use a solution of starch, (1 dessertspoonful to 1 pint of hot water), and dab lightly over the article. Raise the crochet up off the paper, to prevent it sticking as it dries. When dry, remove the pins and press the blouse lightly with a hot iron.

Do not be put off by the little extra trouble necessitated above. When the blouse appears it cannot fail to receive the sincere admiration of friends.

TO MAKE THE BLOUSE
Front
Begin with 209(221; 233)ch.

1st row 1tr into 5th ch from hook, * 5ch, 1ss into 4th ch from hook, 1ch (a picot lp made), miss 5ch, into next ch work 1tr 3ch and 1tr (a V-st made), rep from * omitting V-st at end of last rep, into last ch work 1tr 1ch and 1tr, 3ch, turn.

2nd row Into first 1ch sp work 2tr and 1dc (a half shell made at beginning of row), * a picot lp, into sp of next V-st work 1tr 3ch 1tr (a V-st made over a V-st), a picot lp, into next sp of V-st work 1dc 5tr and 1dc (a shell made over a V-st), rep from * omitting a shell at end of last rep, miss next picot lp, into next sp work 1dc and 2tr, 1tr into next ch (a half shell made at end of row), 4ch, turn.

3rd row 1tr into first tr, * a picot lp, a shell over next V-st, a picot lp, into centre tr of next shell work 1tr 3ch and 1tr (a V-st made over a shell), rep from * omitting a V-st at end of last rep, into 3rd of 3ch work 1tr 1ch and 1tr, 3ch, turn.

4th row A half-shell into first 1ch sp, * a picot lp, a V-st over next shell, a picot lp, a shell over next V-st, rep from * omitting a shell at end of last rep, miss next picot lp, a half shell into next sp, 4ch, turn.

Last 2 rows form patt.

Work in patt for 51 rows more, or length required, ending with a 3rd patt row and omitting turning ch at end of last row. Fasten off.

Armhole shaping
1st row Miss first 3 picot lps, attach thread to centre tr of next shell, 8ch, 1ss into 4th ch from hook, 1ch, a shell over next V-st, work in patt to within last 4 picot lps, a picot lp, 1tr over next shell, 4ch, turn.

2nd row A V-st over next shell, work in patt ending with a V-st over last shell, 1dbl tr into 3rd of 8ch, 1ch, turn.

3rd row 1ss into first tr, 3ch, into sp of same V-st work 2tr and 1dc, a picot lp, work in patt ending with a picot lp, into sp of last V-st work 1dc and 2tr, 1tr into next tr, 4ch, turn.

Work in patt for 15 more rows.

19th row Work in patt until 10 (10, 12) picot lps have been completed, a shell over next V-st, * 5ch, 1dc over next shell, 5ch, 2dc over next V-st, rep from * 1 (2, 1) more times, 5ch, 1dc over next shell, 5ch, a shell over next V-st, work in patt to end.

Neck shaping—first side

1st row Work in patt until 10 (10, 12) picot lps have been completed, 1tr over next shell, 4ch, turn.

2nd row A V-st over next shell, work in patt to end.

3rd row Work in patt ending with a picot lp, into sp of last V-st work 1dc and 2tr, 1tr into next tr, 4ch, turn.

4th row Miss first picot lp, 1tr into next tr, into sp of same V-st work 2tr and 1dc, work in patt to end.

5th row Work in patt ending with a picot lp, into last tr work 1tr 1ch and 1tr, 3ch, turn.

Work in patt for 4 (5, 6), rows more omitting turning ch at end of last row. Fasten off.

Miss 6 (8, 6) lps at centre, attach thread to centre tr of next shell, 8ch, 1ss into 4th ch from hook, 1ch, a shell over next V-st, complete to correspond with first side.

Back

Work as front until 3rd row of armhole shaping has been completed.

Work in pattern for 2 (3, 2) more rows.

Back opening—first side

1st row Work in patt until 13 (14, 15) picot lps have been completed, miss next picot lp, 1dc into next tr, 9ch, turn.

2nd row 1ss into 4th ch from hook, 1ch, a shell over next V-st, work in patt to end.

3rd row Work in patt ending with a V-st over last shell, a picot lp, 1dc into 4th of 9ch, 9ch, turn.

Rep last 2 rows to within last row of front, omitting turning ch at end of last row. Fasten off.

Back opening—second side

1st row Attach thread to first free tr at centre, 1dc into same place as join, a picot lp, a V-st over next shell, work in patt to end.

2nd row Work in patt ending with a picot lp, 1dbl tr into last dc, 1ch, turn.

Complete to correspond with first side.

Sleeves

Begin with 55ch.

1st row 1tr into 5th ch from hook, * a picot lp, miss 4ch, a V-st into next ch, rep from * omitting a V-st at end of last rep, into last ch work 1tr 1ch and 1tr, 3ch, turn.

2nd row As 2nd row of front.

Work in patt for 5 more rows omitting turning ch at end of last row. Fasten off.

Work another section in the same manner ending last row with 3ch, turn.

8th row Work in patt to within last picot lp, a picot lp, into next sp work 1dc and 2tr, join to first section, leaving the last lp

104

of each on hook, work 1tr into 3rd of 4ch on second section and 1tr into last tr worked on first section, thread over and draw through all lps on hook (a joint tr made), into next sp on first section work 2tr and 1dc, a picot lp, work in patt to end (sleeve opening made).

9th row Work in patt working a V-st into joint tr at sleeve opening.

Work in patt for 7 (5, 1) more rows turning with 6ch at end of last row.

Sleeve shaping

1st row 1tr into first tr (a V-st made at beg of row), a picot lp, work in patt ending with a picot lp, a V-st into 3rd of 3ch, 1ch, turn.

2nd row 1dc into first tr, into sp of same V-st work 5tr and 1dc, a picot lp, work in patt ending with a picot lp, into sp of last V-st work 1dc and 5tr, 1dc into 3rd of 6ch, 4ch, turn.

3rd row A V-st over first shell, a picot lp, work in patt ending with a V-st over last shell, 1dbl tr into next dc, 1ch, turn.

4th row 1dc into first tr, into sp of V-st work 5tr and 1dc, a picot lp, work in patt ending with a picot lp, into sp of last V-st work 1dc and 5tr, 1dc into next tr, 4ch, turn.

Rep last 2 rows 3 (3, 2) times more ending last row with 6ch, turn.

Next row A V-st over first shell, a picot lp, work in patt ending with a V-st over last shell, 2ch, 1dbl tr into next dc, 4ch, turn.

Next row 1tr into first dbl tr, a picot lp, a shell over next V-st, work in patt ending with a shell over last V-st, a picot lp, into 4th of 6ch work 1tr 1ch and 1tr, 3ch, turn.

Work in patt for 7 (7, 5) more rows ending last row with 6ch, turn.

Rep from 1st row of sleeve shaping 1 (1, 2) more times ending last row with 4ch, turn.

Work in patt for 13 (15, 13) rows more, or approx 5 cm (2 in.) less than length required ending with a 3rd patt row and omitting turning ch at end of last row. Fasten off.

Shape top

Work as first 3 rows of front armhole shaping.

Work in patt for 3 more rows turning with 1ch at end of last row.

7th row 1ss into first 1ch sp, 4ch, a V-st over next shell, a picot lp, work in patt ending with a V-st over last shell, miss next picot lp, 1dbl tr into next sp, 1ch, turn.

8th row 1ss into first tr, 3ch, into sp of first V-st work 2tr and 1dc, a picot lp, work in patt ending with a picot lp, into sp of last V-st work 1dc and 2tr, 1tr into next tr, 4ch, turn.

9th row Work in patt ending with 1ch, turn.

Rep 7th to 9th rows 5 (5, 6) more times omitting turning ch at end of last row. Fasten off.

Sew side, shoulder and sleeve seams. Sew sleeves into armholes.

Lower edging

1st row With right side facing, attach thread to any side seam, 5dc into each sp, 1ss into first dc.

2nd and 3rd rows 1dc into same place as ss, 1dc into each dc, 1ss into first dc. Fasten off.

Neckband

1st row With right side facing, attach thread to first st on neck edge of back opening, work a row of dc evenly round neck edge having a multiple of 3dc plus 1, 3ch, turn.

2nd row Miss first dc, 1tr into each dc, 3ch, turn.

3rd to 7th rows Miss first tr, 1tr into each tr, 1tr into 3rd of 3ch, 3ch, turn.

8th row As last row ending with 1ch, turn.

Heading

1st row 1dc into first tr, * 6ch, miss 2tr, 1dc into next tr, rep from * ending with 6ch, 1dc into 3rd of 3ch, 7ch, turn.

2nd row 1dc into first lp, * 6ch, 1dc into next lp, rep from * ending with 3ch, 1tr into last dc, 1ch, turn.

3rd row 1dc into first tr, * 6ch, 1dc into next lp, rep from * working last dc into 4th of 7ch, 7ch, turn.

4th row As 2nd row of heading omitting turning ch at end of row. Fasten off.

Right back opening

1st row With right side facing attach thread to top of turning ch on 8th row of neck band, 1dc into same place as join, work a row of dc evenly along edge, 1ch, turn.

2nd row 1dc into each dc, 1ch, turn.

3rd row 1dc into each of first 2dc, 4ch, miss 3dc, 1dc into next dc (button lp made), 1dc into each dc working 1 button lp at base of neck band and 3 button lps evenly spaced along edge and ending with 1ch, turn.

4th row * 1dc into each dc to within next button lp, 4dc into next lp, rep from * ending with 1dc into each dc. Fasten off.

Left back opening

With right side facing, attach thread to first sp at base of opening and work as right back opening omitting button lps.

Cuff bands

1st row With right side facing, attach thread to first sp at lower edge of sleeve opening, work a row of dc evenly along edge having a multiple of 3dc plus 1 and ending with 3ch, turn.

2nd to 7th rows As 2nd to 7th rows of neck band.

8th and 9th rows As last row ending 9th row with 1ch, turn.

Heading

Work as heading for neck band.

Cuff edgings

1st row With wrong side of front edge of cuff band facing, attach thread to first row end, work 18dc evenly along row ends of cuff band, 1ch, turn.

2nd row 1dc into each of first 3dc, 4ch, miss 3dc, 1dc into each of next 6dc, 4ch, miss 3dc, 1dc into each of next 3dc. Fasten off. Attach thread to opposite side and work 18dc evenly across row ends. Fasten off.

Work other cuff to correspond.

Rose motif (make 23)

Begin with 9ch, join with 1ss to form a ring.

1st row * Into ring work 1dc 4tr and 1dc, rep from * 5 more times (6 petals made).

2nd row * Working over last row, into ring work 1dc between last petal and next petal, 6ch, rep from * ending with 1ss into first dc.

3rd row Into each lp work 1dc 1hlf tr 4tr 1hlf tr and 1dc, 1ss into first dc. Fasten off.

Yoke trimming

Begin with 315 (321, 327)ch.

1st row 1tr into 4th ch from hook, 1tr into each of next 64ch, 5tr into next ch, 1tr into each of next 179 (185, 191)ch, 5tr into next ch, 1tr into each of next 66ch, 1ch, turn.

2nd row 1dc into first tr, * 6ch, miss 2tr, 1dc into next tr, ** rep from * working last dc into first tr of next 5tr group, 6ch, 1dc into centre tr of group, 6ch, miss 1tr, 1dc into next tr, rep from first * once more, rep from * to ** working last dc into 3rd of 3ch. 7ch, turn.

3rd to 5th rows As 2nd to 4th row of heading on neck band.

TO MAKE UP

Sew 6 motifs evenly round each cuff band and 11 motifs evenly round neckband.

Sew first row of yoke trimming in position as illustrated.

Sew buttons to back opening and cuff bands to correspond with button lps. Sew overlap at base of back opening. Damp and pin out to correct measurements.

Skirt and bolero

This useful two-piece ensemble (see plate 27) is as pretty as it is practical. It is also quick to make, and quite economical in yarn consumption.

MEASUREMENTS
Bust 91 cm (36 in.)
Waist 66 cm (26 in.)

Hips 96 cm (38 in.)
Length of skirt 53/58 cm (21/23 in.)

MATERIALS

Lee Target Titania double crêpe wool—Light shade 12 balls, Dark shade 9 balls; Crochet hooks 5·00 and 4·50; 3 buttons; 76·3 cm (30 in.) 1·9 cm (0·75 in.) wide petersham ribbon.

TENSION

4sts and 2 rows of treble equal 2·5 cm (1 in.) with 5·00 hook.
Note: Dark shade is referred to as D, Light as L.
Tr 2tog = treble next 2sts by * yoh, insert hook into next st, yoh, pull through 2 lps, rep from * into next st, ending yoh, pull through all lps on hook. Tr 3tog = treble next 3sts tog as follows: work as for tr 2tog, but work repeat into a third st before ending.

TO MAKE THE BOLERO
Back

With No 5·00 hook and L, make 57ch.
1st row   1tr in 3rd ch from hook, 1tr in each ch to end, turn. (56tr).
2nd row   2ch, 1tr in each tr to end, turn.
3rd row   2ch, 2tr in next tr, 1tr in each tr to last 2tr, 2tr in next tr, 1tr in last tr, turn.
4th row   As 2nd row.
Rep 3rd and 4th rows 4 more times, then work 4 rows straight (66tr).

Shape armholes

1st row   Ss across 4sts, 2ch, tr 2tog, 1tr in each tr to last 7tr, tr 3tog, turn.
2nd row   2ch, tr 2tog, 1tr in each tr to last 4tr, tr 3tog, miss turning ch, turn.
3rd row   As 2nd row.
Next row   As 4th row.
Next 10 rows: Work straight.

Shape right shoulder

1st row   2ch, 1tr in next 7tr, tr 3tog, turn.
2nd row   2ch, tr 2tog, 1tr in each tr to end. Fasten off.

Shape left shoulder

Turn and rejoin wool into 11th st from end of last complete row worked.
1st row   2ch, tr 2tog, 1tr in each tr to end, turn.
2nd row   2ch, 1tr in each of next 6tr, tr 2tog. Fasten off.

Right front

With L and No 5·00 hook make 19ch.

1st row   1tr in 3rd ch from hook, 1tr in each ch to end, turn.

2nd row   2ch, 1tr in each tr to last 2tr, 2tr in next tr, 1tr in last tr, turn.

3rd row   2ch 2tr in next tr, 1tr in each tr to last 2tr, 2tr in next tr, 1tr in last tr, turn.

4th row   As 2nd row.

Rep 3rd and 4th rows once more, then work 3rd and 4th rows as given for back three times, then work 4 rows straight. (31tr.)

Shape armhole

1st row   2ch, tr 2tog, 1tr in each tr to last 7tr, tr 2tog, 1tr in next tr, turn.

2nd row   2ch, tr 2tog, 1tr in each tr to end, turn.

3rd row   2ch, tr 2tog, 1tr in each tr until 4sts rem, tr 3tog, miss turning ch, turn.

4th row   As 2nd row.

5th row   2ch, tr 2tog, 1tr in each tr to last 3tr, then tr 2tog, 1tr in next tr, turn.

6th row   2ch, tr 2tog, 1tr in each tr to end, turn.

7th row   2ch, tr 2tog, 1tr in each tr to end, turn.

8th row   2ch, 1tr in each tr to last 3tr, tr 2tog, 1tr in last tr, turn.

Rep 7th and 8th rows twice more, 7th row once again, then work 5 rows straight. Fasten off.

Left front

Work to correspond with right front, reversing all shapings.

TO MAKE UP

Pin out and press according to instructions. Join shoulder and side seams. Press seams lightly.

Edging

With 4·50 hook and right side facing, one round of edging in dc should be worked in L round each armhole and also up right front, round neck, down left front and around lower edge (1dc in each st, 2dc per tr row). Then with right side facing again, 2 more rounds should be worked in D (1dc in each dc), joining each round into beginning with 1ss, and turning between 2nd and 3rd rounds.

Note: Dec at underarm and increase at lower edge of fronts as necessary to keep work flat and curves even.

TO MAKE THE SKIRT

(One piece beginning at waist.)

With No 5·00 hook and L make 98ch.

Foundation rows

1st row   1hlf tr, (1dc, 1dc) into 2nd ch from hook, (1hlf tr in next ch) 3 times, * (1tr in next ch) 3 times, (1hlf tr in next ch) 3 times, ** (1dc in next ch) 8 times, (1hlf tr in next ch) 3 times, rep from * 4 more times and from * to ** once more, ending (1dc in next ch) twice, turn.

2nd row   2ch, * (1hlf tr in next st) twice, 1tr in next st, 2tr in next st, 2dbl tr (1dbl tr, 1dbl tr) in next st, 2dbl tr in next st, 1dbl tr in next st, 2tr in next st, 1tr in next st, (1hlf tr in next st) twice, ** (1dc in next st) twice, ss across next 3sts, 1ch, 1dc in next st, rep from * 4 more times, then from * to ** once more, ending 1dc in last st, dropping L and picking up D, turn.

Note: Always drop wool on hook and pick up new wool at the end of every even numbered row. Carry wool not in use loosely up the side of work.

Pattern rows (chevrons)

1st row   3ch, miss next st, (1tr in next st) 6 times, 2ch, * (1tr in next st) 9 times, miss the slip sts, 1tr in each of next 9sts, 2ch, rep from * to last 8sts, 1tr in each of next 6sts, miss next st, 1tr in last st, turn.

2nd row   3ch, miss next tr, 1tr into each tr to next 2ch lp, * into lp work (1tr, 3ch, 1tr)—a V-st made—1tr into each tr down side of next chevron except last tr, miss this st and first tr of next chevron, 1tr into each tr up side of next chevron to lp, rep from * 4 more times, ending V-st into next lp, 1tr into each tr until 2sts rem, miss next tr, 1tr into last set, turn. (Change wool.)

2nd row forms pattern. All rows are in patt except at shape opening, when details are given. Instructions therefore refer to the only variable—the V-st—which is to be made in one of 3 ways as follows:

1. (1tr, 2ch, 1tr) denoted V1
2. (1tr, 3ch, 1tr) denoted V2
3. (2tr, 2ch, 2tr) denoted V3

Note: All V-sts in the same row are worked in the same way.

3rd row   V3, i.e work in patt working (2tr, 2ch, 2tr) into each lp.
4th row   V2.
5th and 6th, 7th and 8th, 9th and 10th rows   As 3rd and 4th rows.

Shape opening

4ch, 1tr in 3rd ch from hook (2tr increased) 1tr in each tr to next lp, work V3 and patt until last V-st has been worked, then 1tr in each tr ending 3tr into last st, (2tr increased) turn.

12th row   V1
13th row   V1
14th row   V2
15th row   V3
16th row   V1
17th and 18th rows   As 13th and 14th rows.
19th and 20th rows   As 15th and 16th rows.

110

21st row V1
22nd row V1
23rd and 24th rows As 13th and 14th rows.
25th and 26th rows As 15th and 16th rows.
27th to 38th rows As 21st to 26th rows twice. Fasten off.

TO MAKE UP
Pin out and press according to instructions. Join seam from base to bottom of opening (11th row) matching chevrons carefully. Press seam.

Opening edgings
With right side facing and using No 4·50 hook, join D into corner of waist opening and work down to bottom of opening in dc (approx 25dc), turn and work 5 more rows dc. Fasten off. (One flap made for buttons.)

With right side facing, join D to bottom of other side of opening and work up to waist edge in dc to match first side. Turn and work 2 more rows dc. Work a 3rd row missing 1st and making 1ch opposite centre of each of the 2L chevron stripes (2 buttonholes made). Turn and work a 4th row working 1dc into each ch sp. Work 2 more rows to complete as first side (1 flap made for buttonholes).

Waistband
With right side facing and using 4·50 hook, join D into corner of buttonhole flap at waist. Work 6 rows all around waist and across top edges of both flaps, on 3rd row making 1 buttonhole directly above first two.

Sew on buttons to correspond with buttonholes and petersham (approx 2·5 cm (1 in.) longer than correct waist measurement) inside waistband. Cut small hole in petersham behind waistband buttonhole carefully and stitch round buttonhole. Sew bottom edges of flaps together through skirt—button flap inside and buttonhole flap outside.

Skirt and top

Crochet is ideal for separates and plate 28 shows a pattern which will appeal to all ages. Although it has a motif look, it is worked entirely in rows, the spider's web pattern being enclosed in a frame of treble stitches.

MEASUREMENTS
Skirt
Hips 86·91 cm (36 in.)
Waist 56–61 cm (22–24 in.)
Length, excluding fringe 63·5 cm (25 in.) adjustable
Top
Bust 81–86 cm (32–34 in.)

Length from shoulder,
   excluding fringe 33 cm (13 in.)

MATERIALS
Skirt
17 balls Lee Target Duo double crêpe Tricel-with-nylon;
Crochet hooks Nos 2·50, 3·00, 3·50 and 4·00; 68·5 cm (0·75 yd)
elastic, 2·5 cm (1 in.) wide, for waist.
Top
8 balls Lee Target Duo double crêpe Tricel-with-nylon;
Crochet hooks Nos 2·50, 3·00 and 3·50; One button.

TENSION
With No 2·50 hook, 1 patt = 5 cm (2 in.) square
With No 3·00 hook, 1 patt = 5·4 cm (2·12 in.) square
With No 3·50 hook, 1 patt = 5·7 cm (2·25 in.) square
With No 4·00 hook, 1 patt = 6·3 cm (2·5 in.) square

TO MAKE THE SKIRT
Begin at waist—2 pieces
Using No 2·50 hook, make 102ch.
Next row   1dc into 3rd ch from hook, * 1dc into next ch, rep
from * to end, 2ch, turn. (101dc.)
Next row   * 1dc into next dc, rep from * to end, 2ch, turn.
Rep last row 4 times more, increasing 10dc evenly across last
row (by working 2dc into next dc). 111dc.

Begin Pattern
1st row   * 1tr into next dc, rep from * to end, 3ch, turn.
2nd row   1tr into each of next 2tr, * 3ch, (miss 1tr, 1dbl tr into
next tr) 4 times, 3ch, miss 1tr, 1tr into each of next 3tr, rep from
* to end, 3ch, turn.
3rd row   1tr into each of next 2tr, * 3ch, 1dc into each of next
4dbl tr, 3ch, 1tr into each of next 3tr, rep from * to end, 3ch,
turn.
4th row   1tr into each of next 2tr, * 3ch, 1dc into each of next
4dc, 3ch, 1tr into each of next 3tr, rep from * to end, 3ch, turn.
5th row   As 4th row.
6th row   1tr into each of next 2tr, * (1ch, 1dbl tr into next dc) 4
times, 1ch, 1tr into each of next 3tr, rep from * to end, 3ch, turn.
7th row   1tr into each of next 2tr, * (1tr into 1ch sp, 1tr into
next dbl tr) 4 times, 1tr into 1ch sp, 1tr into each of next 3tr, rep
from * to end, 3ch, turn.
The 2nd to 7th rows inclusive from the pattern.
Continue in patt until work measures 10·2 cm (4 in.) from
beginning.
Change to No 3·00 hook and work in patt until work measures
20·3 cm (8 in.) from beginning.
Change to No 3·50 hook and work in patt until work measures
45·7 cm (18 in.) from beginning.

Change to No 4·00 hook and work in patt until work measures 63·5 cm (25 in.) from beginning, ending on completion of a 7th patt row if possible (adjust length here if required).

TO MAKE UP

Pin out and press each piece according to instructions on wrong side. Join side seams. Cut elastic to required waist measurement and join into circle. Work herringbone stitch casing over elastic at inside of waist.

Fringe lower edge by knotting 4 strands of yarn 17·8 cm (7 in.) long into hem, using hook, at approx 1·3 cm (0·5 in.) intervals.

TO MAKE THE TOP

Back

Using No 2·50 hook make 89ch.

Next row 1tr into 4th ch from hook, * 1tr into next ch, rep from * to end. (87tr.)

Now rep 2nd to 7th rows inclusive of patt as given for skirt until work measures 5 cm (2 in.).

Change to No 3·50 hook and work in patt until work measures 17·2 cm (6·75 in.) from beginning, ending after a 6th patt row and omitting turning ch at end of last row.

Shape armhole

Right side facing

Next row 1ss into each of next 2tr, (ss into 1ch sp, ss into dbl tr) 3 times, 3ch, 1tr into 1ch sp, 1tr into next dbl tr, 1tr into 1ch sp, * 1tr into each of next 3tr, (1tr into 1ch sp, 1tr into next dbl tr) 4 times, 1tr into 1ch sp, rep from * 4 times more, 1tr into each of next 3tr, (1tr into 1ch sp, 1tr into dbl tr) twice, turn.

Next row 1ss into each of next 2tr, 3ch, 1tr into next tr, * 1tr into each of next 3tr, 3ch, (miss 1tr, 1dbl tr into next tr) 4 times, 3ch, miss 1tr, rep from * to last 7sts, 1tr into each of next 5tr, turn.

Next row 1ss into each of next 2tr, 3ch, 1tr into each of next 2tr, * 3ch, 1dc into each of next 4dbl tr, 3ch, 1tr into each of next 3tr, rep from * to last 2sts, 3ch, turn.**

Now work 3 rows in patt, beginning with a 4th patt row.

Make back opening

Right side facing

Next row 1tr into each of next 2tr, * (1tr into 1ch sp, 1tr into next dbl tr) 4 times, 1tr into 1ch sp, 1tr into each of next 3tr, rep from * once more, 2ch, miss ch sp and 1dbl tr, 1tr into next ch sp, 1tr into next dbl tr, 3ch, turn.

Next row 1tr into next tr, 2ch, miss 2ch sp, patt to end (as 2nd patt row).

Continue in patt keeping 2tr and 2ch at opening edge as set until work measures 35·6 cm (14 in.) from beginning, (ending after a

7th patt row). Fasten off.

Return to sts for other side, rejoin yarn to top of first dbl tr at centre and work 2ch, 1tr into 1ch sp, 2ch, miss 1dbl tr and ch sp, patt to end.

Continue in patt to correspond with other side to end.

Front

Work as back as far as **

Now work in patt beginning with a 4th patt row until work measures 31·8 cm (12·5 in.) from beginning, ending after a 2nd patt row.

Shape neck

Next row   1tr into each of next 2tr, 3ch, 1dc into each of next 4dbl tr, 3ch, 1tr into each of next 3tr, 3ch, turn.

Now work 4 rows in patt on these sts, beginning with a 4th patt row. Fasten off.

Return to sts for other side, miss 3 patts at centre, rejoin yarn to first of next 3tr 2ch, patt to end.

Continue in patt to correspond with other side to end.

TO MAKE UP

Pin out and press each piece on wrong side according to instructions. Join shoulder and side seams. Fringe lower edge as for skirt.

Armhole edging

With right side facing and using No 3·00 hook, rejoin yarn and work 2 rows dc evenly round armhole edges.

Next row   *Miss 1dc, (1dc, 2ch, 1dc) into next dc, rep from * all round. Fasten off.

Neck edging

With right side facing and using No 3·00 hook, rejoin yarn to left corner of back neck opening and work 1 row dc round neck, down right edge of opening and up left edge. Work a further row dc round neck to corner, 2ch, miss 2dc, 1dc into next dc, (buttonhole lp made), work in dc down right edge and up left edge of opening to corner.

Next row   (work along neck edge only), * miss 1dc, (1dc, 2ch, 1dc) into next dc, rep from * to end. Fasten off. Sew button to left corner of opening.

Press all seams and edgings.

Flower-motif waistcoat

Printed by kind permission of the designer, Elizabeth Collins, and *Woman's Realm* magazine. The waistcoat is illustrated in plate 29.

This garment, modelled in Associated Television's *Woman*

Today Crochet Party programme, produced by Jean Morton, is an eye-catcher wherever it goes. The raised clusters and bobble edging provide an unusual and striking look.

Three sizes, from 81 cm (32 in.) to 91·25 cm (36 in.) bust, can be made simply by changing the size of the hook used for the motifs.

MEASUREMENTS

Bust	81 cm	86·25 cm	91·25 cm
	(32 in.)	(34 in.)	(36 in.)
Length from shoulder	61 cm	63·5	66 cm
	(24 in.)	(25 in.)	(26 in.)

MATERIALS

Emu Tricel nylon double knitting			
Dark shade	9	9	10 balls
Medium shade	8	8	8 balls
Light shade	5	5	6 balls
Crochet hook	4·00	4·50	5·00

Note: A cluster is worked thus: work 4tr, remove hook from lp and insert it through first tr and through lp, then draw one lp through.

D = Dark colour; M = Medium colour; L = Light colour.

THE MOTIF (Make 31)

With D, make 4ch, join with 1ss to form ring.

1st round 3ch, 3tr into ring, remove hook from lp, insert through 3rd of 3ch and through the lp, then draw the lp through, (3ch, 1cl into ring) 3 times, 3ch, 1ss into top of first cl. Fasten off.

2nd round Join L to any 3ch sp, then work (1dc, 4tr, 1dc) into every 3ch sp, 1ss into first dc. (4 petals.)

3rd round * 4ch, then taking hook behind the next petal, work 1dc into the 3ch sp, (i.e. inserting hook between 2nd and 3rd tr of petal and working into the 3ch sp of round 1), 4ch, 1dc into back of work between the petals, rep from * 3 times, but finish with 1ss into first st. (8 4ch sps.)

4th round (1dc, 4tr, 1dc) into every 4ch sp, 1ss into first dc. Fasten off L, and join in M.

5th round 1dc into every st to end, 1ss into first dc. (48dc.)

6th round 5ch, * miss next st, 1dc into next st, 1ss into next st, 1dc into next st, 3ch, miss 3 sts, 1dc into next st, 1ss into next st, 1dc into next st, 1ch, miss next st, 1dbl tr into next st, 1ch, rep from * 3 times, but finish with 1ss into 4th of 5ch instead of 1dbl tr.

7th round Ss into first 1ch sp, 3ch, 2tr into same sp, * 1ch, (1cl, 1ch) 4 times into next 3ch sp, 3tr into next 1ch sp, 1ch, 3tr into next 1ch sp, rep from * twice, 1ch, (1cl, 1ch) 4 times into next

3ch sp, 3tr into next 1ch sp, 1ch, ss into top of 3ch.

8th round   2ch, 1hlf tr into each of next 2tr, * 1dc into top of each of next 4cls, 1hlf tr into each of next 3tr, (2hlf tr, 2ch, 2hlf tr) into next 1ch sp, so forming a corner, 1hlf tr into each of next 3tr, rep from * twice, 1dc into each of next 4cls, 1hlf tr into each of next 3tr, (2hlf tr, 2ch, 2hlf tr) into next 1ch sp, 1ss into top of the 2ch. Fasten off.

9th round   Join in D. Work 1dc into every st and (2dc, 2ch, 2dc) into each corner 2ch sp.

10th round   As 9th round. Fasten off.

TO COMPLETE

Press work on wrong side with a cool iron over a slightly damp cloth. To join first 2 squares, place them together with right side inside, then using D work a row of double crochet through both thicknesses all along the edge. Arrange the squares as shown in Fig. 41 and join together; then join shoulders, matching A–B to A–B, C–D to C–D.

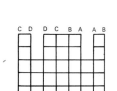

Fig. 41. The layout for the squares for the flower-motif waistcoat.

Border

With right side facing join D to lower edge at one side seam.

1st round   2ch, 1hlf tr into same place as join, (yoh, insert hook into sp just formed between 2ch and hlf tr, and draw a lp through) 3 times (7 lps now on hook), yoh, miss 1dc, insert hook in next dc, draw a lp through, yoh and draw a lp through first 2 lps on hook, yoh and draw a lp through first 7 lps on hook, yoh and draw a lp through rem 2 lps * (yoh, insert hook into sp just formed at base of 'bobble', and draw a lp through) 3 times, yoh, miss 1dc, insert hook in next dc and draw a lp through, yoh and draw a lp through first 2 lps on hook, yoh, and draw a lp through first 7 lps on hook, yoh, and draw a lp through rem 2 lps, rep from * all round, but work 2 bobbles into corner st at lower edge of each front, 1ss into top of 2ch.

2nd round   2ch, 1hlf tr into same place as ss, (yoh, insert hook into sp between 2ch and hlf tr, and draw a lp through) 3 times, yoh, insert hook in next 1ch sp and draw a lp through, yoh, and draw a lp through first 2 lps on hook, yoh and draw a lp through first 7 lps on hook, yoh and draw a lp through rem 2 lps, * (yoh, insert hook into sp at base of bobble, and draw a lp through) 3 times, yoh, insert hook in next 1ch sp, and draw a lp through, yoh, and draw a lp through first 2 lps on hook, yoh, and draw a lp through first 7 lps on hook, yoh, and draw a lp through rem 2 lps, rep from * all round, but work 3 bobbles at each corner, 1ss into top of 3ch. Fasten off.

Work sleeve edging to match, but work only the first round of border.

Press carefully.

Plate 28 (*Above*) The lacey skirt and top.

Plate 29 (*Top right*) The flower-motif waistcoat.

Plate 30 (*Right*) The coloured-motif doily—this would brighten any room.

Plate 31 (*Above*) Tri-colour, Tunisian-crochet tunic.

Plate 32 (*Below left*) Three-colour dip pattern.

Plate 33 (*Below centre*) Three-colour mosaic pattern.

Plate 34 (*Below right*) Chevron pattern in two colours.

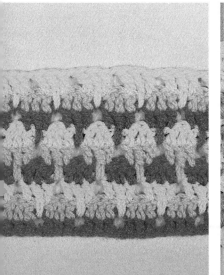

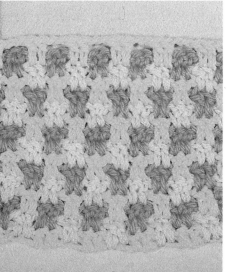

Trolley cloth

This type of cover is used extensively in these days of meals in comfort by the fireside. It is reasonably quick and easy to make. Any shades of Mercer cotton can be used for the pretty floral sprays and triple leaf motifs which are applied to the cloth (see Fig. 42).

This idea can also be carried out on a larger cloth or smaller set of table mats. When applied to fashionwear it can add a touch of distinction.

MATERIALS
2 Balls Coats Mercer Crochet No 40 (20 gm); 45·5 cm (0·5 yd) old bleach coloured linen 91·25 cm (36 in.) wide; Steel crochet hook No 1·00.

MEASUREMENTS
43 cm (17 in.) × 55·5 cm (22 in.)

FLORAL SPRAY
Main stem
Begin with 60ch, 1dc into 10th ch from hook, working over cord

Fig. 42. The trolley cloth.

(or 4 strands of same thread), work 1dc into each ch making 5dc into last ch (base of stem), 1dc into each ch along opposite side, 1dc into ring. Fasten off.

Flower—first petal
Begin with 20ch.

1st row 1dc into 2nd ch from hook, 1dc into each ch to within last ch, 3dc into last ch, 1dc into each ch along other side of foundation, 1ch, turn.

2nd row Picking up back lp only, work 1dc into each dc to within 3dc at tip, 2dc into each of next 3dc, 1dc into each rem dc, 4ch, turn.

3rd row * Miss next 3dc, 1dc into next dc, 4ch, rep from * 3 times more, * miss 2dc, 1dc into next dc, 4ch, rep from last * twice more, * miss 3dc, 1dc into next dc, 4ch, rep from last * twice more, 1dc into last st. Fasten off.

2nd petal Work same as first petal until 2nd row is complete, turning with 1ch.

3rd row 1dc into corresponding lp on first petal, 2ch, miss 3dc on 2nd petal, 1dc into next dc, 2ch, 1dc into corresponding lp on first petal, 2ch, miss 3dec on 2nd petal, 1dc into next dc, 4ch, and complete as for first petal.

Make 3 more petals, joining as before.

With right side of work towards you, holding downward, attach thread at base of first petal. Work dc across base of petals, keeping centre curved. Now work 1 row of dc and 1 row of tr along these dc, decreasing on each row to keep necessary curve for centre. Working along side of petals, work 4dc into each lp to within tip, 5dc into each of 3 lps at tip, 4dc into each of next 2 lps, 2dc into next lp, 2dc into next lp on next petal, and continue thus all round completing last petal to correspond. Fasten off.

Rose centre
Begin with 15ch, join with 1ss to form a ring.

1st row * 6ch, 1dc into ring, rep from * 4 times more.

2nd row Into each lp work 1dc 1hlf tr 1tr 8dbl tr, 1tr, 1hlf tr and 1dc, 1ss into sp formed by original ring at base of rose petal. Into each sp at base of petals work 1hlf tr 5tr and 1hlf tr. Break off, leaving a 10 cm (4 in.) thread and fasten to centre of petal section.

Sew to top of main stem.

Single rose
Work as for rose centre and fasten off at end of 2nd row.

Triple leaf
Begin with 15ch, and hereafter work over a cord (or 4 strands of same thread).

1st row 1dc into 2nd ch from hook, 1dc into each ch to within last ch, 5dc into last ch, 1dc into each ch along opposite side of foundation, 3dc over cord only.

Hereafter pick up only the back lp of each dc: 1dc into each dc to within 4dc from centre dc at tip of leaf, 1ch, turn.

2nd row 1dc into each dc to within centre of 3dc (over cord), 3dc into centre dc, 1dc into each dc on other side to within 4dc from centre dc at tip of leaf, 1ch, turn.

3rd row dc to within centre of 3dc group, 3dc into centre dc, dc on other side to within last 3dc, 1ch, turn.

4th to 6th rows As 3rd row. Fasten off.

Make 2 more leaves like this. Sew sides of leaves together to form a triple leaf.

TO MAKE THE CLOTH

Floral spray. Work 1 floral spray as instructions.

Small spray. Work a single rose and 1 stem and a small rose same as floral spray.

Twig. Begin with 15ch. Working over cord, work 1dc into 2nd ch from hook and into each ch across. Fasten off.

Triple leaves. Now work sufficient triple leaves (20) to go all round edge of cloth.

TO MAKE UP

Cut linen 37 cm (14.5 in.) × 49.5 cm (19.5 in.). Withdraw a thread 0.5 cm (0.25 in.) from edge all round.

Work a row of double crochet all round working into spaces of drawn thread. Sew floral sprays and leaves in position as illustrated.

Dampen and press.

Coloured-motif doily

Looking for all the world like a posy of flowers from a tropical sea, this gay motif doily will bring a sunny look to any sitting room, no matter how dull the day. See Fig. 43 and plate 30.

MATERIALS

1 ball each Coats Mercer Crochet No 20 (20 gm): Rose Madder, Light Marine Blue, Emerald Green, Amber Gold, Shaded Lavender and White. Other shades may of course be used according to personal preference. Crochet hook No 1.25.

MEASUREMENTS

Size of motif = 3.75 cm (1.25 in.)
Size of doily = 35.5 cm (14 in.)

TO MAKE THE DOILY
First motif
With Amber Gold, begin with 6ch.

Fig. 43. A section of the coloured motif doily showing the linked motifs and edging.

1st row 1tr into 6th ch from hook, (2ch, 1tr into same ch) 4 times, 2ch, miss 2 of 6ch, 1ss into next ch.

2nd row 1dc into same place as last ss, * 3 dc into next sp, 1dc into next tr, rep from * ending with 3dc into last sp, 1ss into first dc. Fasten off.

3rd row Attach Light Marine Blue to same place as last ss, 3ch, 1tr into same place, * 7ch, miss next 3dc, 2tr into next dc, rep from * ending with 7ch, 1ss into 3rd of 3ch.

4th row 1dc into same place as last ss, 1dc into next tr, * 9dc into next lp, 1dc into each of next 2tr, rep from * ending with 9dc into last lp, 1ss into first dc. Fasten off.

Make first 2 rows on all motifs in Amber Gold.

Second motif

Work same as first motif until 3rd row is completed, using White on 3rd row in place of Light Marine Blue.

4th row 1dc into same place as last ss, 1dc into next tr, 5dc into

120

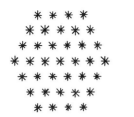

Fig. 44. Positioning the motifs for the doily.

next lp, ss into centre dc of any lp on first motif, 4dc into same lp on second motif, 1dc into each of next 2tr, 5dc into next lp, ss into centre dc of next lp on first motif, 4dc into same lp on second motif. Complete as for first motif.

Make 35 more motifs in assorted colours (excluding Emerald Green), joining adjacent sides as previous motifs were joined. (See Fig. 44 for position of motifs.)

Ruffle

1st row Attach Emerald Green to any dc on edge of doily, 4ch, 1dbl tr into back lp of each dc all round outer edge of motifs, 1ss into 4th of 4ch.

2nd row 7ch, * miss next 2dbl tr, 1dbl tr into next dbl tr, 3ch, rep from * ending with 1ss into 4th of 7ch.

3rd row 1ss into each of next 2ch, 8ch, * 1dbl tr into next sp, 4ch, rep from * ending with 1ss into 4th of 8ch.

4th and 5th rows Ss to centre of sp, 9ch, * 1dbl tr into next sp, 5ch, rep from * ending with 1ss into 4th of 9ch.

6th row 7ch, 1dbl tr into same place as last ss, * 5ch, into next dbl tr work 1dbl tr 3ch and 1dbl tr, rep from * ending with 5ch, 1ss into 4th of 7ch.

7th row * Into next sp work 2dc 4ch and 2dc, into next sp work 3dc 4ch and 3dc, rep from * ending with 1ss into first dc. Fasten off.

Starch and pin out to measurement.

Tri-colour, Tunisian-crochet tunic

This snug, firm-textured classic tunic with long sleeves, high neck and belt is eminently suitable for colder-weather wear over slacks or a skirt (see plate 31).

Printed by kind permission of *Woman and Home* magazine.

MEASUREMENTS

Bust	81 cm (32 in.)	86·25 cm (34 in.)	91·25 cm (36 in.)	96·5 cm (38 in.)
All round at underarms	85 cm (33·5 in.)	90·5 cm (35·75 in.)	96·25 cm (38 in.)	102 cm (40·25 in.)
Side seam (including edging)	48 cm (19 in.)	48 cm (19 in.)	48 cm (19 in.)	48 cm (19 in.)
Length (including edging)	68·5 cm (27 in.)	69 cm (27·25 in.)	69·5 cm (27·5 in.)	70·25 cm (27·75 in.)
Sleeve seam (including edging)	42·5 cm (16·75 in.)	42·5 cm (16·75 in.)	42·5 cm (16·75 in.)	42·5 cm (16·75 in.)

MATERIALS

Patons Totem double
  crêpe in 50-gm balls

Main Colour	7	7	7	8 balls
1st Contrast	4	5	5	5 balls
2nd Contrast	4	5	5	5 balls

1 No 3·5 and 1 No 5 Tunisian crochet hook; 1 No 3·00 crochet hook; 5 buttons.

TENSION

With No 5 Tunisian hook.
21 sts 10 cm (4 in.) in width
8 rows 2·5 cm (1 in.) in depth over Tunisian Simple stitch.

TO MAKE THE TUNIC

Note: The instructions are given for the 81 cm (32 in.) bust size. Where they vary, work the first figure within the brackets for the 86·25 cm (34 in.) bust, the second bracketed figure for the 91·25 cm (36 in.) bust, and the third for the 96·5 cm (38 in.) bust.

The back

With No 3·5 Tunisian crochet hook and Main Colour (M), make 98(104; 110; 116)ch. Do not break off yarn.
Join in First Contrast (C1) and change to No 5 hook, and with C1 work the first foundation row of Tunisian Simple st (see page 76)
Do not break off C1, join in Second Contrast, and work the 2nd foundation row.
Now continuing in Tunisian Simple st, in stripe sequence of 1 row M, 1 row C1 and 1 row C2, work 12 rows straight.
Continuing in stripes as set, dec at each end of the next row and the 4 following 8th rows thus: insert hook under 2 vertical lps, yoh, and draw lp through. [88(94; 100; 106)sts.]
Work 89 rows straight.

To shape armholes

Next row   Work in dc as for finishing (see page 75) across 4 sts, then patt as usual until 4 remain.
Work 1 row back, then dec at each end of next row and the 6(7; 8; 9) following alt rows. 66(70; 74; 78)sts.**
Work 43 rows straight.

To shape shoulders

Next row   Work in dc as for finishing across 7 sts, then patt as usual until 7 remain.
Work 1 row, then rep these 2 rows once more.
Next row   Work in dc as for finishing across 5(6; 7; 8), then

patt as usual until 5(6; 7; 8) remain.
Work 1 row back across the 28(30; 32; 34) rem sts, then work one dc row and fasten off.

The front
Work as given for back until ** is reached.
Work 23 rows straight.
Now divide sts for neck.
Next row Patt 26(27; 28; 29) and then slip these sts on to a stitch holder until required for left front shoulder, work in dc as for finishing across the next 14(16; 18; 20)sts for neck, then work in patt to end. Now continue on these 26(27; 28; 29)sts for right front shoulder.

Right front shoulder
Work 1 row back, then dec at neck edge on next row and 6 following alt rows 19(20; 21; 22) sts.
Work 5 rows straight.***
For shaping continue thus:
Next row Patt until 7 remain.
Work 1 row back, then rep these 2 rows once more.
Work in dc for finishing across the rem 5(6; 7; 8)sts. Fasten off.

Left front shoulder. Rejoin appropriate coloured yarn to inner edge of sts left on stitch holder. Slip sts back on to hook and work as given for right front shoulder to ***.
For shaping continue thus:
Next row Work in dc as for finishing across 7sts, patt to end as usual.
Work 1 row back, then rep these 2 rows once more.
Work in dc for finishing across the rem 5(6; 7; 8) sts. Fasten off.

The sleeves (both alike)
With No 3.5 Tunisian hook and M, make 44(46; 48; 50)ch. Do not break off M. Join in C1, change to No 5 hook and with C1 work the first foundation row of Tunisian Simple st. Leave C1 hanging, join in C2, and work the 2nd foundation row.
Continuing in Tunisian Simple st in stripe sequence as for back, work 10 rows straight.
Continuing in stripes as set, inc 1st at each end of next row and the 9 following 10th rows, thus: insert hook between 2 vertical lps, yoh, and draw lp through.
On the 64(66; 68; 70)sts work 15 rows straight.

Shape sleeve top
Next row Work in dc as for finishing across 4sts, then patt as usual until 4 rem.
Work 1 row back, then dec at each end of next row and the 15(16; 17; 18) foll alt rows. (24sts.)
Work 1 row back.

Next row Work in dc across 3sts, patt until 3 rem.
Work 1 row back, then rep these 2 rows once more.
Work in dc for finishing across the 12 rem sts. Fasten off.

The lower edgings (back and front alike)
With right side of work facing, rejoin M, and using No 3·00 hook, work 98(104; 110; 116)dc along lower edge, then turn and work 11 rows of dc over dc. Fasten off.

Sleeve edgings (both alike)
With right side of work facing, rejoin M, and using No 3·00 crochet hook, work 44(46; 48; 50)dc along lower edge, then turn work and work 11 rows of dc over dc. Fasten off.

The neckband
First join right shoulder seam. With right side of work facing, rejoin M, and using No 3·00 crochet hook, work 17dc down left front neck edge, 14(16; 18; 20)dc across front neck edge, 17dc up right front neck edge, and 28(30; 32; 34)dc across sts of the back neck edge. [76(80; 84; 88)dc.]
Work 11 rows dc over dc. Fasten off.

The belt
With No 3·00 crochet hook and M, make 143(153; 163; 173)ch and work as follows:
1st row 1dc into 2nd ch from hook, 1dc into each ch to end, turn.
Work 11 rows dc over dc. Fasten off.

TO MAKE UP
Press all parts on the wrong side with a warm iron over a damp cloth. Join left shoulder seam for 1·25 cm (0·5 in.) at armhole edge. Set in sleeves. Join sleeve and side seams. Lightly press seams.

The left shoulder opening
With right side of work facing, rejoin M to top of neck band at back and, using No 3·00 crochet hook, work 12dc along row ends of neck band and 16dc along back shoulder edge, then 16dc along front shoulder edge and 12dc up row ends of front neck band, turn. (56dc.)
Next row 2ch to stand for first dc, 1dc into next dc, *miss 2dc, 2ch, then 1dc into each of next 5dc, rep from * 4 times, then work dc to end, turn.
Next row Work in dc, working 3dc into each ch sp. Fasten off.
Sew on buttons.

Part 3
Learning to Crochet

First principles

METHODS OF LEARNING

Crochet work appears to the uninitiated to be complex in structure, yet it is a fact that every pattern emerges from just a few simple basic stitches. Before attempting anything more than a practice piece these stitches must be thoroughly mastered. Then, and only then, will they be evenly formed, flowing in easy rhythm from the ball through hook and nimble fingers.

Successful pattern-reading, or design, cannot be accomplished until the worker can differentiate between each stitch. Once this fluency of movement and recognition is achieved, anything the hook can do may be tackled with complete confidence.

Most crochet work grows from a foundation row or ring of chain stitches. To the experienced crocheter this holds no difficulties, but the beginner inevitably appears to have problems from the very first loop.

Two methods of learning have been devised by the author. Both of these overcome this early difficulty, eliminating frustration by by-passing entry into a foundation chain until the basic stitches are thoroughly mastered. Each method substitutes a more substantial basis upon which to build the various stitches, and gives early enlightenment on turning chains and end-stitches, which confuse so many learners.

The first system, known as the *Winne method* uses a comb-like gadget into which the yarn is threaded. The basic stitches are learned one by one by entry into a row of spaces. Figure 45 shows the Winne threaded in readiness for action.

The complete Winne outfit, 'Crochet for Beginners', manufactured by J. W. Spear & Sons Ltd, of Enfield, Middlesex, is available at most leading stores, needlework, toy, and some book shops.

The second method is the *double crochet foundation*, which is fully explained in this section of the book. It is based on a foundation row of double-crochet stitches which provides a more substantial first row than the series of unevenly formed chain

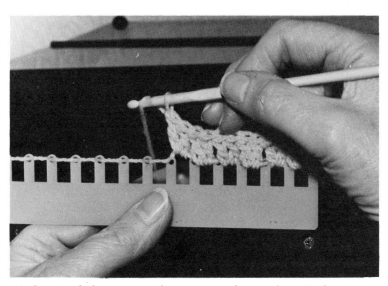

Fig. 45. The Winne crochet aid, threaded for use.

stitches made by a somewhat tense and apprehensive beginner.

As in any skill, there are numerous rules to be learned. These will be fully explained later. Of far more importance at this stage is a close study of the basic stitches.

Left-Handed Workers

'Lefties' will be relieved to know that it is equally easy to crochet either the right- or left-handed way. In fact the author herself, although naturally a 'lefty', has always worked 'righty' with crochet.

For those who simply cannot consider working as for the right, instructions for the left are given in brackets after those for the right. A small mirror propped up opposite the right-handed instruction diagrams will assist in their translation.

During the lessons, the usual abbreviations for crochet terms, adopted for convenience of printer and worker, will be shown the first time each appears. Thereafter, they will be used in the text, giving a gradual insight into this very important side of crochet.

BASIC EQUIPMENT

Three things only are necessary to begin learning:

1. A medium-sized crochet hook, preferably size 5·00, 4·50 or 4·00.

2. A ball of quite thick yarn; either double crêpe or a slightly thicker yarn is excellent for this purpose.

3. A little concentration, in quiet surroundings if possible.

It is very important to develop from the beginning a completely relaxed hold on hook and yarn. Tense fingers and wrists will never produce anything but difficult, tight work; it is far better to work *very* loosely at first. With either method of learning, good tension will develop naturally as the stitches are practised.

128

TENSION

Tension means the number of stitches, or patterns, and rows to a given measurement and 'pay attention to your tension' should be the slogan of every crochet worker. Yet all too often the tension test is considered unnecessary and is by-passed in the hope that all will be well in the end.

All designs are based on the particular tension figures mentioned in the printed pattern. To neglect making the test is to risk ultimate failure in an exercise where good fortune is unlikely to be on your side.

To obtain correct tension, work the piece as instructed in the pattern. Press lightly where necessary, and mark out very carefully with knob pins the exact measurement over which the test is to be taken. If there is so much as a fraction of a stitch too many, then a hook a size larger should be used to repeat the test. If a fraction of a stitch too few appears within the pinned boundary, then a size smaller hook should be used for a further test piece. In other words, if the tension test says 6 stitches to 2·5 cm (1 in.) and your figure is 6½ stitches, or 5½ stitches, the final result after working the fabric with the wrong tension figure, on a 45·5 cm (18 in.) piece of work would be 49·5 cm (19·5 in.), or 43 cm (16·5 in.).

Among crocheters, tension varies so much that it is sometimes necessary to use a hook one, two, or even three sizes smaller, or larger; to produce material of correct tension.

HOOKS

The beginner should be conversant with hook sizes, and on page 130 is a list of hooks made today to the International Standard range of sizes adopted by all major European manufacturers. As many people still use hooks of the older sizes, these appear alongside the International sizes.

Figure 46 illustrates in actual size the hooks now being used in crochet patterns, providing an adequate number of sizes to work present-day and older patterns.

Tunisian (Afghan) hooks

These hooks are made in various lengths, some of the longer types being made in several sections which are screwed together to form one long hook. Each hook has a knob at one end to prevent the stitches falling off and there is no flattened holding section along the stem. (See Fig. 47.)

The sizes conform to the International Range as for ordinary hooks.

Fig. 47. A Tunisian (Afghan) hook.

Hairpin

Hairpin crochet, described on page 70, uses a special U-shaped

Fig. 46. Crochet hooks shown actual size.

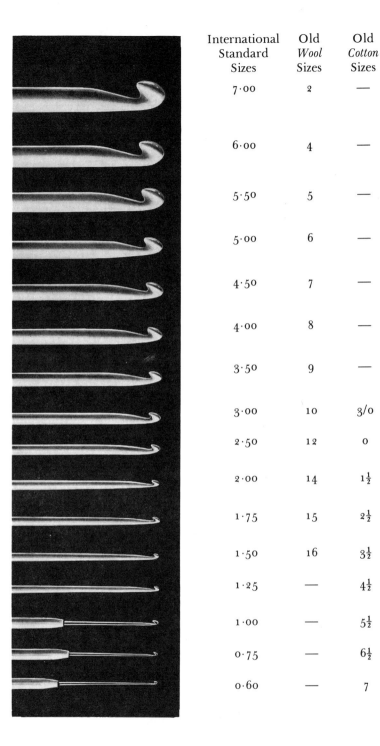

International Standard Sizes	Old *Wool* Sizes	Old *Cotton* Sizes
7·00	2	—
6·00	4	—
5·50	5	—
5·00	6	—
4·50	7	—
4·00	8	—
3·50	9	—
3·00	10	3/0
2·50	12	0
2·00	14	$1\frac{1}{2}$
1·75	15	$2\frac{1}{2}$
1·50	16	$3\frac{1}{2}$
1·25	—	$4\frac{1}{2}$
1·00	—	$5\frac{1}{2}$
0·75	—	$6\frac{1}{2}$
0·60	—	7

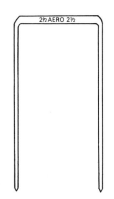

Fig. 48. The U-shaped tool used for hairpin crochet.

tool (see Fig. 48) in conjunction with the hook to produce gimps of varying widths and lengths which can be joined together to make a variety of articles.

Metric and equivalent English sizes are given below:

METRIC	ENGLISH
—	$\frac{1}{2}$ in.
20	$\frac{3}{4}$ in.
25	1 in.
30	$1\frac{1}{4}$ in.
35	—
40	$1\frac{1}{2}$ in.
45	$1\frac{3}{4}$ in.
50	2 in.
60	$2\frac{1}{2}$ in.
70	—
80	3 in.
100	—

WINNE TEACHING AID

The teaching aid, patented by the author, and described on page 127 is made in one size only in slightly flexible plastic. (See Fig. 49.)

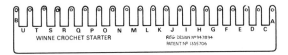

Fig. 49. The Winne teaching aid.

Basic techniques

THE STARTING LOOP

Take the end of the yarn over the hook, under the yarn from the ball and into the hook (Fig. 50). Pull the hooked yarn through the loop (lp) on the hook, holding the knot firmly between thumb and first finger of left (right) hand. The starting lp is now on the hook, and should slide easily along the hook stem.

THE HOLDING POSITION

Hold the hook, at the flattened part of the stem, pencil-wise in the right (left) hand between thumb and first finger, with starting lp on hook. In the left (right) hand hold the starting knot between thumb and first finger (Fig. 51).

Now thread the yarn from the lp over the first three fingers of left (right) hand and under the fourth. (There are various ways of achieving a holding position. For beginners and with thicker yarns this one is excellent.) See Fig. 52.

An alternative hold of the yarn takes it right round the little finger, under the third and over the second and first (Fig. 53).

Fig. 50. Making the starting loop.

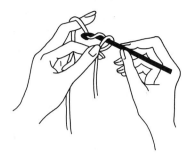

Fig. 51. The holding position for the hook and starting loop.

Fig. 52. The holding position for the yarn—first method.

Fig. 53. The holding position for the yarn—second method.

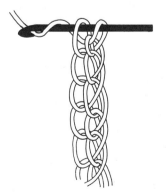

Fig. 54. The double-crochet foundation row.

This hold is recommended for the finer yarns.

In both these holds the second finger with yarn over it is raised slightly, for it is *under* this thread that the hook will take the yarn. The temptation to take the hook over this thread should be avoided at all times (knitters are very prone to this!).

WORKING IN ROWS
The double crochet (dc) foundation row

With lp on hook and in correct holding position, take yarn over hook (yoh), and pull this through lp on hook—1 chain (ch) made. Yoh again, and pull this through lp on hook—2nd ch made.

Note: Throughout crochet work, always move the holding thumb and first finger of the left (right) hand along directly underneath each new stitch being made. If this is practised from the beginning it very quickly becomes a habit.

When working, try to cultivate the habit of pulling *down* with the left (right) hand holding thumb and finger, and pulling *up* with the right (left) hand hook-holding fingers. The second hook-holding finger should rest comfortably behind the first.

Inspection of the starting lp will reveal three strands of yarn. Insert hook under two of these, yoh, and draw through lp just picked up (2lps on hook), yoh, and draw through 2lps on hook, (1lp now on hook), 1dc made.

* Insert hook into lp at extreme left (right), yoh, and draw through lp just hooked, yoh again, and draw through both lps on hook *, 2nd dc made.

Repeat (rep) from * to * up to 10 times. (See Fig. 54.)

Note: Beginners will probably find this first attempt unevenly formed. Undo it down to the slip lp and rep again and again until the stitches (sts) are well formed and flow rhythmically from the hook.

To work a row of double crochet stitches (sts) over the foundation row

Note: When working in rows, the right-handed work from right to left, the left-handed from left to right.

Begin with a perfectly formed dc foundation row. Holding it horizontally between thumb and first finger of left (right) hand, under last st of the row, take the yarn from the work over the first three fingers of left (right) hand and under the fourth, which should be bent right over to control the flow of yarn. Hold the hooked lp in right (left) hand.

Now tilt foundation row slightly forward, and at the top of each foundation dc st will be seen a neat row of ch sts. Into each of these make 1dc, as follows:

Insert the hook under both sides of very first top ch st, yoh, and draw the hook back through st just picked up, (2lps on hook),

132

yoh and pull through both lps on hook (1dc made); * insert hook under both sides of next top ch st, yoh and draw back through st just picked up, yoh, and pull through both lps on hook * (2nd dc made). Rep from * to * to end of foundation row.

Note: If a 10dc stitch foundation row was worked, there should now be 10dc sts over this row.

Figure 55 shows the ch st picked up and yoh ready to be taken back through both lps on hook.

Now unravel your work, and rep from end of dc foundation row until a perfect row of dc sts has been worked into the foundation.

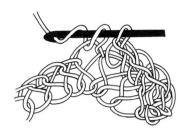

Fig. 55. Double-crochet stitches over the foundation row. The chain stitches are on the hook in preparation for the formation of the next stitch.

Turning the work

Before proceeding further it is advisable to become acquainted with procedure at the end of the row. These vital end-stitches can then be practised as the other basic stitches are learned.

When working in rows, the work has to be turned round at the end of one row so that the reverse side is facing the worker, in preparation for the new row to be made.

In plain fabric, chain stitches are usually added at the end of one row to prepare for the next. These are called 'turning chains', and their number varies according to the stitch with which the new row begins. The following is a general guide, although the number of turning chains may vary according to a particular pattern.

To prepare for double crochet (dc)

Usually no ch to turn, as the first dc of the new row is worked into the very first st. Sometimes 1ch is made at end of row, and the first st of the new row is missed.

To prepare for half treble (hlf tr)

2ch to turn, forming first st of new row.

To prepare for treble (tr)

3ch to turn, forming first st of new row. Sometimes this is reduced to 2ch to give a firmer edge.

To prepare for double treble (dbl tr)

4ch to turn.

To prepare for triple (trip), quadruple (quad) and quintuple (quin) tr

5ch, 6ch and 7ch, respectively.

Half treble

Make a dc foundation row as before. Turn this to horizontal position.

In order to prepare for the row of hlf trs to follow, it will be necessary to make 2ch sts to form the first st, thus: yoh, and draw through lp on hook, yoh again, and draw through lp on hook (2ch made).

To make the first half tr
Ignoring st at base of ch just made, * yoh, and insert hook under both sides of next top ch st, draw this through new ch st just picked up, (3lps now on hook), yoh again and draw this thread through all 3lps on hook *. This leaves 1lp on hook, and the first hlf tr is made.

Rep from * making 1 hlf tr into each top ch st of previous row, *not forgetting the last st.* There should now be the same number of sts along the row as on the dc foundation, counting the 2 turning ch as the first st of the row.
Note: When working straight, always count the sts very carefully, making sure not to miss the last st of every row.

Figure 56 shows the 2 turning ch sts marked with odd lengths of yarn, and the hook about to take yarn through all 3 lps on hook for the 4th hlf tr st.

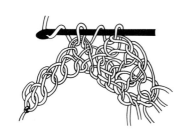

Fig. 56. Forming a half-treble stitch.

Treble
Make a dc foundation row as before, and make 3 turning ch (t ch).

Ignoring st at base of this ch, * yoh, insert hook under both sides of next top ch st, yoh, and draw through st just picked up, (there are 3lps now on hook) yoh again, and draw through first 2lps on hook, yoh again and draw through last 2lps, (1lp now on hook) * 1tr made. Rep from * to * making 1tr into each dc foundation st to end.

Figure 57 shows 3lps on hook, yoh ready to take off the first 2lps. The three odd strands of yarn indicate the t ch. 3tr have already been made.

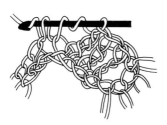

Fig. 57. Forming a treble stitch.

Double treble
Make a dc foundation row as before, then 4t ch. Ignoring st at base of t ch, * yoh twice, insert hook into next top ch st, yoh, and draw through st just picked up, (4lps on hook), yoh again, and draw through first 2lps on hook, yoh, and draw through next 2lps on hook, yoh and pull through last 2lps on hook, (1lp now on hook), * 1dbl tr made. Rep from * to * to end of foundation row.

Figure 58 shows the 4t ch marked with odd strands of yarn, 3dbl tr already made, and yarn hooked twice, new st picked up and yoh ready to take off first 2lps for 4th dbl tr.

Triple, quadruple and quintuple trebles
These are all made similarly to dbl trs, except that before beginning to make the st, the yarn is hooked 3, 4 or 5 times respectively, and the lps taken off the hook two at a time in the same manner.

Fig. 58. Forming a double treble.

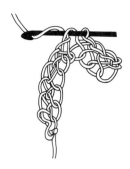

Fig. 59. Forming a slip stitch.

Slip stitch (ss)
No turning ch is made in this case. * Insert the hook into first top ch st of dc foundation row, yoh, and, holding down work very firmly, pull this thread through both lps on hook (1ss made). Rep from * to end of foundation row.

Figure 59 shows new st picked up by hook, and yoh ready to be taken through new st and lp in one movement.

These basic stitches form the foundation of all crochet work. Practise them well until each individual stitch is well-formed and easily recognized.

FASTENING OFF
To fasten off last stitch of work, break off the yarn a few cm (in.) from the last stitch made, yoh, draw through lp on hook, pull thread right through lp. Pull up stitch slightly and sew end neatly into work.

WORKING INTO A CHAIN FOUNDATION
Rows of dc
Make a slip loop as explained on page 131; 20 ch. Now work exactly as for the first row of dc into dc foundation row, but begin by taking into the hook two of the three threads of every ch st to end of foundation ch. There will be 20dc in the row.

Making no t ch, work a further ten rows of dc, working 1dc into every dc of previous row. Figure 60 shows section of plain dc fabric.

Fig. 60. A section of plain double-crochet fabric.

Rows of hlf tr
Work as above, making first hlf tr into 2nd ch from hook, and l hlf tr into every foundation ch. (There will be 20sts including first t ch.) For second row, make 2t ch, and proceed to work a further ten rows of hlf tr. Figure 61 shows a section of plain hlf tr fabric.

Fig. 61. A section of plain half-treble fabric.

Rows of tr

Work as above, making first tr into 3rd ch from hook, and 1tr into every foundation ch. (There will be 19sts including first t ch.) For second row and others make 3t ch, and proceed to ten rows of tr. Figure 62 shows a section of plain tr fabric.

Fig. 62. A section of plain treble fabric.

Rows of dbl tr

Work as before, making first dbl tr into 4th ch from hook, and 1dbl tr into every foundation ch to end. There will be 18sts including first t ch. For second row make 4t ch, and proceed to ten rows of dbl tr. Figure 63 shows a section of plain dbl tr fabric.

Fig. 63. A section of plain double-treble fabric.

Fig. 64. The 6-chain basis for the circle.

Fig. 65. The chain joined with a slip stitch into a circle.

WORKING FROM A PATTERN

You are now ready to tackle a simple pattern worked in rows. Do not be too ambitious at first. The patterns on page 14, 32, 36 and 42 make very good 'starters'.

WORKING IN CIRCLES

When working in circles or squares, right-handers work each round in an anti-clockwise direction, left-handers in clockwise manner.

THE CHAIN FOUNDATION

There are several ways of beginning crochet in the round, but the chain foundation provides the best basis for learning.

TO BEGIN

Make 6ch, join to first ch with 1ss to form a circle. See Figs 64 and 65.

Work 8dc right into the ring, not into each individual ch st (Fig. 66). Join with 1ss to complete the round.

Fig. 66. The first round of the circle. Double-crochet stitches have been worked into the ring.

Next round Work 2dc into each dc of previous round, join with 1ss to complete round.

Further rounds Work 2sts into 1, as required in order to keep the circle lying flat.

Note: Make a habit of marking with a small safety pin or a piece of contrasting yarn, the first st of each new round, moving it up as each round is completed.

INCREASING AND DECREASING
To increase one stitch
To increase one stitch during the course of a row, simply work twice into the same stitch. If an increase is to be made at the beginning or end of a row, the neatest way to do this is to work twice into the second, or next-to-last stitch of the row.

Figure 67 (top) shows 1tr increase in second stitch of second row, 1tr increase in centre of row, and 1tr increase in second stitch from end of row.

To increase more than one stitch at the beginning of the row
Make the number of chain stitches representing 1ch for each increase, and add to this the number of chains required for the turn, i.e., if the increase is to be 4tr and 2 turning chains are required, the total number of extra chains required is 6, the first stitch being made in to the 3rd ch from hook.

To increase more than one stitch at the end of the row
Preparation for the increases will have to be made at the beginning of the row previous to the increase row. This is done by working the number of chains required, plus the necessary tur-

Fig. 67. The piece of work at the top shows 1 treble increase in the second stitch of the second row, 1 treble increase in the middle of the row and 1 treble increase in the second stitch from the end. The work at the bottom shows 4 treble increases at the beginning of the row and the slip stitches at the end over which the increase will be worked.

137

ning chains, then slip stitching over these for the increase stitches. The result will form the first stitches of the row. The increased stitches at the end will be made over the slip stitches of the previous row, thus keeping in line with the increased stitches at the beginning of this row. Figure 67 (bottom) shows 4tr increase at the beginning of the row, and the slip sitches at the end over which the increases will be worked.

To decrease by one stitch
Double crochet
When working in dc, all that is necessary is to miss one stitch wherever the decrease is to be made. Figure 68 (top) shows hook missing one stitch and inserted into the next stitch.

Treble
Work one tr into stitch, leaving last loop on hook, (half-closed tr) make another half-closed tr into next st, yoh, and draw through all 3 loops on hook (1tr dec made).

Fig. 68. To decrease by 1 stitch (top) in double-crochet work and (middle) in treble-crochet work. The piece of work at the bottom shows how to decrease by more than 1 stitch.

Figure 68 (middle) shows 2 half-closed tr loops on hook, and yoh in readiness to draw through all 3 loops on hook.

To decrease by more than one stitch
At the beginning of a row, simply work the number of slip stitches over the required number of decreases, then work the usual turning chain, and continue along the row.

At the end of a row, leave unworked the requisite number of stitches to be decreased, make the usual turning chains, and continue working the next row.

Figure 68 (bottom) shows 2tr dec at beginning and end of row, with 2 turning ch ready for next row.

CROCHETING IN MIXED COLOURS
Colour attracts, and crochet emphasizes this fact. See plates 25 and 33 for examples showing the blending of assorted colours to give eye-catching results.

Three-colour dip pattern
This is shown in plate 32.
1 row is worked in each colour, and repeated throughout.
Begin with a length of chain divisible by 4 plus 3.
1st row Into 3rd ch from hook 1tr, 1tr into each of next 2ch, 1ch, miss 1ch, * 1tr into each of next 3ch, 1ch, miss 1ch, rep from * to last 3ch, 1tr in each ch, 2ch, turn.
2nd row * 1tr in each of 3tr, 1ch, rep from * ending with 1tr, 2ch, turn.
3rd row * 1tr in tr, 1ch, miss 1tr, 1tr in next tr, 1dbl tr inserting hook in 1ch sp of first row between tr gps, rep from * ending with 1tr, miss 1st, 1ch, 1tr in end tr, 2ch, turn.
4th row As 2nd row beg with 1tr, 1ch.
5th row 1tr in 1st tr, * 1dbl tr in 1ch sp between tr of 3rd row, 1tr in next tr, 1ch, miss 1st, 1tr in next tr, rep from *, ending with 1dbl tr, and 1tr in last tr.
6th row As 2nd row, ending with 3tr.

Three-colour mosaic pattern
Begin with a length of chain.
1st row With first colour 2ch, * 2tr, 2ch, miss 2sts, rep from *, ending with 2tr.
2nd row With second colour, * 2ch, 2tr in 2 missed sts of 1st row over 2ch sp, rep from *, ending 2ch, 1dc.
3rd row With third colour, 1ch, * 2tr in 2tr of first row, 2ch, rep from *, ending with 2tr.
4th row With first colour repeat 1st row, working tr in tr of 2nd row.
Continue in sequence as required.
This pattern is shown in plate 33.

139

CHEVRON PATTERN

See plate 34.

Begin with a length of chain in multiples of 14 + 12

1st row   6dc, *3dc in next st, 5dc, miss 3sts, 5dc, rep from * for required number of times, ending with 6dc, turn.

2nd row   Miss first dc, *5dc, 3dc in next st, 5dc, miss 2sts, rep from *, ending with 6dc.

Rep 2nd row as required, working stripes as designed.

SOLOMON'S KNOT

This is shown in Fig. 69 and is a favourite for light texture.

1st row   Begin with slip lp, 1ch, *draw up lp to 1·5 cm (0·5 in.) or length required, yoh, and draw through into a loose ch st, insert hook under two of the 3 lps of ch st just made, yoh, and draw through both lps on hook, making the knot. Rep from * for length required, make 2 more knots, turn.

2nd row   Into 3rd knot work 1dc, * work 2 knots, work 1dc into next knot of previous row. Rep from * working 1dc at end of row into first ch of first row, make 2 knots, turn.

3rd row   Work 1dc into 4th knot from hook and continue working as 2nd row, making last dc into centre of turning sts.

Further rows   Rep 3rd row.

Last row   Rep 3rd row with knots to match 1st row.

Fig. 69. Solomon's knot.

Fig. 70. To make twisted cord: *A* At each end make a knot and insert a pen or similar object. *B* Twist in a clockwise direction. *C* Bring the ends together and let the cord twist round itself.

Note: Hold loop firmly each time to prevent slipping before knot is made.

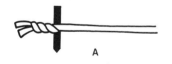

TWISTED CORD

Invoke the aid of a friend for this if possible; if not fix the end to a door handle or chair leg during the twisting operation.

For a dress belt, double-quality yarn or thicker qualities give very good results. The cord can be made in any thickness with any number of strands.

The cord

Measure 6, 8 or more 5 metre (5·5 yds) lengths of yarn. Knot the ends together, inserting a pen or other similar object at each

Fig. 71. To make a pom-pom, two circles of card like this are required.

Fig. 72. Thread yarn around the card circles with a blunt-ended needle.

Fig. 73. Cut the yarn at the outer edge, between the card circles.

Fig. 74. Knot the securing cord around the pom-pom.

end in front of knot (Fig. 70A). Keeping the wool for twisting straight out, holding the end by the pen, turn clockwise (Fig. 70B). Continue turning until there is a tight twist along the cord. Bring pens together and let the cord twist round itself (Fig. 70C). Slip out the pens and knot ends together.

POM-POMS

An outfit for making pom-poms manufactured by J. W. Spear & Sons Ltd, Enfield, takes the fiddling out of cardboard cutting to size. This is available at most leading stores and handicraft and toy shops.

If the kit is not available, cut two 6·5 cm (2·5 in.) circles of cardboard, and make a 1·25 cm (0·5 in.) hole in the centre of each, with a slit (Fig. 71).

Place the circles together and thread a blunt-ended needle with a long length of double or treble strands of yarn. Thread this yarn round the circles of card until the centre cavity is filled (Fig. 72).

With a really sharp pair of scissors, cut round the outer edge of circles, between the cards (Fig. 73), and then tie a length of yarn very tightly around the centre. Knot securely, remove the cards, neaten by clipping the pom-pom (Fig. 74).

Do not cut off the tied ends, as these will be used to tie to the ends of the cord, or other article for which the pom-poms are made (Fig. 75).

Fig. 75. Twisted cord with a pom-pom at each end.

General hints

SHAPING

'Steps' as a result of decreasing cannot always be avoided in crochet, due to the depth of the rows. If a straight seam is used when joining up, these will not appear.

Neck shaping

The way to eliminate 'steps' when working the first row of the neckband or edging, is to insert the hook within the step to form a good, even curve.

Borders and edgings

A smaller sized hook and missing one stitch at even intervals will produce a firm edge.

MISTAKES

When an error in working has occurred the only way to rectify it is to unravel to the point where it happened, and continue working again.

TO SHORTEN CROCHET WORK

If a garment, or other article, has dropped, or if fashion decrees a shorter hemline or sleeve, run a piece of contrast yarn through the row immediately below the line of the new hemline. With scissors, cut through every stitch which joins this row to the one above, then take away all loose threads. Finish off neatly. (See Fig. 76.)

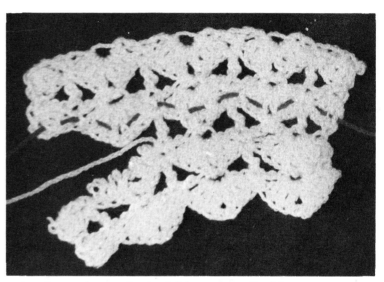

Fig. 76. Shortening crochet work.

An alternative method, which works well with some patterns, is to measure the exact length required, and at the end of a row cut the thread which connects the two rows. Take hold of the thread and pull the stitches undone along the row. Finish off as required.

JOINING YARN

There are several ways of doing this. When working in rows it is always advisable to make the join (never a knot) at the end of a row several centimetres (inches) before the end of the ball.

Place the end of the used ball along the top of the next stitches to be worked. Loop over the hook the end of the new ball, and work over the old and new ends to secure them.

When working in stripes, 'steps' will be avoided if the last loop of the last stitch of the row is worked in the new colour.

To join a new colour some distance from the first, as in the Old American Square, insert the hook into the new position, loop the yarn over and draw through the stitch, then work 1 chain stitch using double yarn, and continue working with new yarn. Fasten off the odd end securely. (See Fig. 77.)

Fig. 77. Joining yarn.

COUNTING THE ROWS

It is always rather tedious counting the rows, and one row is easily forgotten. A row-counter takes the worry out of this proceeding, and should be used whenever possible.

TIPS

When working straight, make certain always to work into the first and last stitch of every row.

Always work selvedge stitches evenly, firmly and neatly; this leads to perfect seams later.

When making up, never stretch the edges as they are being taken together.

Yarn from a new ball should always be joined at the end of a row, even if it means wasting a length of thread. This end can be used later during making-up.

A new colour should be joined at the last yoh of previous row, thus forming the first loop of next row.

When working in rounds it is usual to complete each round with a slip stitch into the first stitch of that round, and to begin the next round with the appropriate number of chain stitches to form first stitch.

To avoid needle-threading when fastening off ends at sides of work, insert a crochet hook in one loop of several stitches along the side edge, yoh, and draw the end through.

When applying crochet squares or other shapes to material, they must be laid perfectly flat, tacked first into position then sewn neatly with tiny, invisible stitches instead of the more usual overcasting, thus giving a neater outline.

Making-up can be done very effectively by joining together both sides with a row of slip stitches or double crochet on the wrong side. This not only gives a neat, invisible seam, but is quickly undone if necessary at a later date, without the risk of cutting through a wrong thread.

If joining the piece of a garment worked in thick yarn, neater seam will be produced by dividing the thread.

Foundation rows may be formed in double crochet or treble stitches instead of the usual chain, particularly when the first row is designed in one of these stitches.

An ever-ready quick measure may be made by marking the stem of the crochet hook in centimetres, using a tiny spot of nail varnish or other suitable semi-permanent colouring matter.

Buttons should always be made, or bought, slightly larger in size than the buttonhole worked.

For a neat finish and better fit on neckline, pants or bra, several rows of shirring elastic woven just inside the edges on the wrong side will give the desired effect.

When calculating yarn requirements, it is always advisable to err on the generous side. In case of unfortunate underestimating, always keep one of the ball bands with the work for matching-up purposes.

Remember, when adjusting measurements given in a printed pattern, to adjust proportionately the quantities of yarn stated.

Never hang garments in a wardrobe. In a roomy drawer they will rest comfortably without crease or drop.

Always take extra care when making up. A little more time spent on this all-important stage of the work will be rewarded by the final result.

Care of crochet work

WASHING

When possible use soft water. Rain water is not often available or suitable. Domestic water can be softened by the addition of one tablespoonful bicarbonate of soda to 100 grammes of yarn. The water should be slightly warmer than lukewarm, never hot, otherwise the fabric may be damaged.

Washing powders and other preparations should be thoroughly dissolved and mixed before the article is immersed. Several rinsings in water of equal temperature to the first should be used to free the article from all lather.

After washing, place between two towels and roll quite tightly, without squeezing, to remove as much moisture as possible.

Drying should take place with the garment lying perfectly flat after being eased into the correct size.

Pressing instructions, usually printed on the ball band should always be followed implicitly.

DRY CLEANING

It is always advisable to pin a note to the item to be cleaned specifying the type of yarn from which it is made. Draw the attention of the cleaner to this, in case special care is needed during processing.

Index